EVERYTHING

YOU NEED TO KNOW ABOUT...

Gluten-Free
Cooking

EVERYTHING

YOU NEED TO KNOW ABOUT...

Gluten-Free Cooking

RICK MARX AND NANCY T. MAAR

David and Charles

A DAVID & CHARLES BOOK

amendments copyright © David & Charles Limited 2006

Copyright © 2006 F+W Publications Inc.

& Charles is an F+W Publications Inc. company
4700 East Galbraith Road
Cincinnati, OH 45236

First published in the UK in 2006
First published in the USA as *The Everything® Gluten-Free Cookbook*,
by Adams Media in 2006

A catalogue record for this book is available from the British Library.

ISBN-13: 978-0-7153-2492-9 paperback
ISBN-10: 0-7153-2492-6 paperback

Printed in Great Britain by CPI Bath
for David & Charles
Brunel House   Newton Abbot   Devon

Visit our website at www.davidandcharles.co.uk

David & Charles books are available from all good bookshops;
alternatively you can contact our Orderline on 0870 9908222 or
write to us at FREEPOST EX2 110, D&C Direct, Newton Abbot,
TQ12 4ZZ (no stamp required UK only).

*In light of the complex, individual and specific nature of health problems, this book is not intended to
replace professional medical advice. The recipes in this book are intended to supplement, not replace, the
advice of a trained medical professional. While the authors and publisher have made every attempt to
offer accurate and reliable information to the best of their knowledge and belief, it is presented without
any guarantee. The author and publisher therefore disclaim any liability incurred
in connection with the information contained in this book.*

Contents

Acknowledgments

To those who helped with the creation of this book, Rick Marx wishes to thank Judy Lynch, who first raised our awareness to the needs of coeliac disease sufferers; Pat MacGregor, chairperson, Gluten-Free Restaurant Awareness Program and Westchester Celiac Sprue Support Group board member, for generously sharing time and information; Alessio Fasano, M.D., professor of paediatrics and director of paediatric gastroenterology and nutrition and medical director, Center for Celiac Research; Dr. Audrey Birnbaum, M.D., a physician affiliated with Northern Westchester Hospital in Mount Kisco, New York; and Kathy Garrett for her articles on gluten-free diet for the *Record-Review*.

Nancy Maar thanks her husband, Leonard Maar, for helping with the recipes and for acting as test taster, and friends at St Paul's on the Green in Norwalk, Connecticut, for sharing the gluten-free chocolate cheesecake. She thanks her children, who are always happy when she is doing what she loves!

To our agent, June Clark, for her belief in the project and ability to make it happen, and to editor Kate Burgo and all the great people at Adams Media.

Introduction

As anyone who has tried to adapt to a world that is not geared toward gluten-free eating knows, a kitchen or a restaurant can be a treacherous experience, with dangers at every turn. Each ingredient and product must be scrutinized and analysed, and a safe approach must be developed. People who are gluten intolerant – among them, the millions who suffer from coeliac disease and food allergies – know that they must read the labels on not only the obvious potential offenders but also foods that the uninitiated might not even think twice about. Staple ingredients such as soy sauce, malt vinegar, some dairy products, and some brands of baking powder may contain gluten.

Fortunately, alternative ingredients derived from rice, corn, and other sources can be found in markets or ordered easily online. It is our goal to serve those who require a gluten-free lifestyle and help maintain their sanity, to develop a delicious and practical approach to dining while eliminating the elements that are detrimental to health or that may create adverse reactions.

Our goal has been to work with easy-to-use, everyday ingredients readily found in most supermarkets, organic markets and health food stores. In some cases, the more exotic ingredients may need to be sought on the Web at some of the many excellent stores geared to those with coeliac disease or food allergies.

We provide answers for those who enjoy the pleasures of everyday food and cooking and seek to create a well-balanced, tasty menu of delicious recipes for themselves. We have tried to avoid the most exotic entrées, although hopefully we have provided some interesting and useful recipes to help you create a healthy diet.

As we have found, building up a gluten-free kitchen and lifestyle is not a solo enterprise. Cooperation among family members, friends, or housemates can be an essential component of the gluten-free lifestyle. To that end, we have sought to provide delicious dishes that appeal not only to those who are required to avoid gluten, but to those who do not have any such intolerance. The best compliments we've received are from those who have enjoyed our meals not because they are gluten-free, but because they are simply delicious.

We've divided this book up into a wide variety of gluten-free selections. We offer recipes for meat, fish, poultry, and vegetarian dishes, along with soups, varieties of corn and rice. Condiments and sauces play an important role in making the dinner table come alive, and we've included a wide variety of chutneys, salsas and more. We've also put together breakfast and dinner choices for everyday cooking pleasures. You'll be able to plan a dinner party for friends, and you'll find ways to enjoy cooking for kids. Whatever your favourite dish, you'll discover new recipes and ways of having fun in the kitchen, whether by yourself, with family or entertaining. New options are available every day, as ingredients become easier to acquire and the Internet brings support groups and friends closer.

Awareness of gluten allergies and the desire for a healthier diet have led to an interest in and a demand for quality gluten-free food. Gluten-free dining groups have formed, and motivated individuals seek to bolster their knowledge and access to gluten-free recipes and materials. *Everything you Need to Know about Gluten-Free Cooking* is an easy-to-use guide to cooking healthy, delicious gluten-free meals and treats.

Measurement Conversions

Liquids

¼ cup	=	60ml	=	2fl oz
⅓ cup	=	80ml	=	2 ½fl oz
½ cup	=	125ml	=	4fl oz
⅔ cup	=	150ml	=	5fl oz
¾ cup	=	180ml	=	6fl oz
1 cup	=	250ml	=	8fl oz

Dry Goods

1 cup:

apricots, dried	125g	=	4oz
breadcrumbs, fresh	80g	=	2 ¾oz
dried	100g	=	3 ½oz
cheese, grated Parmesan	100g	=	3 ½oz
grated Cheddar	125g	=	4oz
ricotta	250g	=	8oz
chickpeas, dried	220g	=	7oz
chocolate, grated	125g	=	4oz
chips	185g	=	6oz
cocoa	85g	=	3oz
cornmeal	185g	=	6oz
courgettes, diced	125g	=	4oz
cranberries	125g	=	4oz
cranberries	125g	=	4oz
crisps, crushed	60g	=	2oz
fish, cooked, diced	150g	=	5oz
flour,			
(wheat)	125g	=	4oz
buckwheat	185g	=	6oz
chestnut	150g	=	5oz
cornflour	125g	=	4oz
maize	185g	=	6oz
potato	220g	=	7oz
rice	150g	=	5oz
tapioca	150g	=	5oz
herbs, fresh, whole	30g	=	1oz
chopped	60g	=	2oz
lentils	250g	=	8oz
meat, cooked, diced	150g	=	5oz
mushrooms, chopped	85g	=	3oz
nuts, chopped	125g	=	4oz
olives, chopped	185g	=	6oz
peas, frozen	125g	=	4oz
rice, uncooked	220g	=	7oz
cooked	185g	=	6oz
spinach, raw, chopped	60g	=	2oz
spring onions, chopped	90g	=	3oz
sugar, caster, granulated	250g	=	8oz
icing	125g	=	4oz
sultanas	150g	=	5oz

Chapter 1

Understanding Gluten-Free Cooking

Many people don't know much about gluten-free diets until they find out they need to be on one. Unless you or someone you know suffers from coeliac disease or has serious food allergies, you may not be aware of exactly what gluten-free cooking involves. This chapter covers the basics of what you need to know about this diet.

Why a Gluten-Free Diet?

Is a gluten-free diet important for your lifestyle? If you have a food allergy or the autoimmune disorder known as coeliac disease, it may be important for you to take charge of your life and begin a new food regimen.

About 1 in 133 people suffer from coeliac disease, and health organizations say 2–2.5 per cent of the general population suffer from food allergy – or 1–1.5 million people in Britain. The difference between food allergy and coeliac disease is that the latter, also known as coeliac sprue, is an autoimmune disorder, like diabetes.

Unlike other autoimmune diseases, however, doctors know the trigger for coeliac disease: gluten, which provokes an immune response that causes the body to attack itself. Two key components come into play in coeliac disease: genes and environmental factors.

Coeliac disease is an intestinal disorder caused by the intolerance of some individuals to gluten, a protein that is found in wheat, rye, barley and some other grains. Gluten irritates the intestinal lining, interfering with the absorption of nutrients and water. Unlike certain food allergies, coeliac disease is not 'grown out of', and those with the disease must maintain constant vigilance to keep their diet gluten-free. Untreated, the disease can lead to severe complications and potential long-term illness. The disease is permanent, and damage to the small intestine will occur every time gluten is consumed, regardless of whether symptoms are present. Reactions among people who suffer from this disease vary, but they are inevitable. The only treatment is strict adherence to a 100 per cent gluten-free diet.

Diagnosis of coeliac disease starts with blood testing, in which doctors study the series of antibodies that provide a good marker of the tendency to have the illness. Blood testing is often followed up with an intestinal biopsy.

Maintaining a healthy gluten-free lifestyle involves eating a well-balanced, gluten-free diet that is high in protein and normal in fats. Common nutrient shortages among people with coeliac disease include deficiencies in calcium, the vitamin B complex and vitamins A, C, D, K and E. It is important for the coeliac sufferer to eat a carefully balanced diet to ensure that he or she is getting all the vitamins the body needs.

What Can I Eat?

The gluten-free diet involves totally eliminating the ingestion of all items containing the proteins found in wheat, rye, barley and the many related grains. Before you turn to a gluten-free diet, make sure you see your doctor and determine if eliminating gluten is right for you. Starting the diet without complete testing is not recommended and makes subsequent diagnosis more difficult. Always be safe rather than sorry.

Once you've made the decision to be gluten-free, you can purchase ingredients at natural food stores, online and at some supermarkets. Fresh fruits, meats and veggies are a great place to start – always remember, if they are fresh, they are gluten-free. If the food is processed or prepared, the chances are it is not. In building a gluten-free diet plan, remove wheat grain products, including the obvious – breads, cakes, and scones – and the not so obvious – among them, products with wheat starch or other gluten-containing grain derivatives.

Every person with coeliac disease must become a bit of a chemist. Preparing delicious gluten-free foods takes practice, diligence and experimentation. Audrey Birnbaum, M.D., a physician affiliated with Northern Westchester Hospital in Mount Kisco, New York, who specializes in paediatric gastrointestinal disorders and food allergies, recommends purchasing products on the Internet or from health food stores, and enlisting the assistance of a dietitian. She says that it's usually easy to make the whole family comfortable with a gluten-free diet.

'Try to stay as pure as possible,' Dr. Birnbaum says. 'Is it OK to cheat? I tell patients: Bring your own gluten-free cupcakes. You don't have to be obsessive, but you should be an intelligent consumer.'

That includes reading labels, checking websites, and staying informed on medical developments. Some supplements may be required to replace the nutrients lost by eliminating wheat and gluten from the diet. For example, the body's iron requirements might go up.

Nutritionist Renee Simon recommends adhering to the four *R*'s of eating:

- Remove foods that are unhealthy.
- Replace these with ingredients that are important for your nutrition.
- Rejuvenate, with exercise and healthy living.
- Repair your body with a steady and healthy dietary regimen.

Even with the gluten-free food sections available in stores, shopping can be a hassle. You must still read every label very carefully. Preparing meals can take a lot of effort, especially at first. By eating fresh foods, stocking up on the right ingredients, absorbing basic information, and building up your recipe file, you can start benefiting from a gluten-free diet in as little as one day, or in up to six weeks. Supplements like echinacea, to boost the immune system, garlic, which is an antibacterial, vitamin C and Chinese herbs can also be useful in helping you live a healthy life.

Gluten-Free for Kids

Coeliac disease can appear at any age, and can be seen in children as young as one year old. Some doctors are conducting research that could connect gluten and food allergies to other diseases and syndromes, for example, autism and Asperger's syndrome. They are seeking to determine if there might be a way to manage those kinds of disorders using a gluten-free or casein-free diet.

Once you make the decision to replace gluten, 'It's a life experience, and it's a life-changing experience,' says Pat MacGregor, member of a coeliac gluten-free support group. 'I was determined my daughter wasn't going to suffer. If other kids had pizza and cookies, she was going to have pizza and cookies.'

At home, you can watch what your kids eat. At school and outside, it's not so easy. Education, planning, and vigilance are important for establishing and maintaining a safe school environment. Try providing your kids with a lunch box containing their favourite foods and drinks or encourage them to carry gluten-free dried fruits or raisins in a bag. Make sure they understand that they shouldn't swap food with their friends.

Parents can plan for a gluten-free lifestyle by talking to their child's school. Support organizations can provide an educational pack of information for the parents of allergic children, which can be helpful in informing teachers and other staff about your child's needs, keeping them alert to dangerous situations that could lead to an allergic reaction. Schools do not currently have to provide gluten-free meals, though some school caterers may be willing to make small changes that ensure their food is safe, and you may prefer to provide packed lunches for your child.

'It's really important to us that my son is treated as "Benjamin" and not treated as "the boy with food allergies",' says a parent of a young child with coeliac disease. 'Everybody has something to deal with in their lives – this happens to be his.'

The emphasis on making sure your child stays safe and healthy while keeping his or her school life as average as possible is of the greatest importance. Letting your child be part of the group is also at the top of the priority list.

Eating Out

Gluten-free dining out can be very difficult. When at a restaurant, making the requirements of a gluten-free meal clear to a waiter or chef is a complicated process. Change the dynamic with a new eating approach. Instead of reading the menu and seeing all the good things that you *can't* have, look for all the good things you *can* have. Mentally eliminate the pasta, the sandwiches, the gravy and sauces, and anything that looks complicated. Some soy sauces may contain gluten. Many restaurant sauces have gluten in them, and sometimes the beef and chicken are prepared and vacuum packed in a stock that contains gluten. A salad may come with croutons. You'll also need to avoid anything breaded or battered. Other pitfalls are French fries, onion rings, chicken wings and other foods that have been dusted with flour.

If you are extremely sensitive, don't take anything for granted. The chef might know whether something on the menu is gluten-free, but the waiting staff most likely will not.

Like Pat, consider starting a restaurant group in your area. It can provide companionship, moral support, and be the source of delicious meals and recipes. Pat works with restaurant owners and chefs to design a programme where group members meet once a month to get together and eat a gluten-free meal. Find restaurants that can work with you. Rather than fume at what they *can't* do, work with chefs and managers to prepare a menu that works for you. (They may even teach you a few great new meals!)

There are a few chains that have developed gluten-free menu additions, among them McDonald's and Outback Steakhouse. They can easily be located in advance when you're planning a trip.

Living a Gluten-Free Lifestyle

Most large supermarkets and, particularly, specialist health food stores carry a variety of gluten-free foods. Visit your local store or go to the Web. Talk to friends or support groups who have had experience with coeliac disease or food allergies. Find out all the different flours you can use, and maximize the resources at your fingertips.

To put together a gluten-free store cupboard, make sure you have four kinds of flour. We recommend rice, maize, chestnut (for desserts) and quinoa (for protein). You'll need an electric blender, a mixer and a food processor, items that any cook would find useful but that are essential for the preparation of gluten-free food. Stock up on plenty of fresh vegetables, lots of good meats, and high-quality seafood. Avoid preseasoned foods, as flour may have been added to the seasoning mix.

Scott Adams, founder of celiac.com and the Gluten Free Mall in the USA, offers an online site that sells a wide variety of gluten-free products. Scott, who has coeliac disease, started the business in 1996 to give consumers greater options in buying gluten-free products. Scott recommends that consumers prepare their lists by consulting support groups and doing research at home and online. His site and others, such as coeliac.co.uk, often provide links to manufacturers, products and product information.

The EU allergen labelling directive, which came into effect in 2005, provides consumers with valuable information about what goes into the preparation of foods they buy. All ingredients, including additives, flavourings and processing aids, have to be listed, and known allergens are shown in a separate box on the label.

- When in a supermarket or grocery store, make sure you read the labels.
- Open your mouth and ask questions everywhere you go.
- Once you've gone gluten-free, don't hesitate to share your new food lifestyle.

Cook for friends and family. Coauthor Nancy Maar took a gluten-free chocolate-mint cheesecake to share with the parishioners at her church. 'I said, "This is gluten-free," and everyone said, "That's fine; I'll try it." It went fast! Most of those people didn't care whether the food had gluten or not – they just wanted it to taste good.'

Don't feel deprived – gluten-free food is as delicious as any other. For example, food fried in deep fat in the style of the American south has no wheat flour – it's made with maize flour and/or cornmeal. Dip meat, chicken, vegetables and prawns in maize flour and egg, then in cornmeal, and you've got a crunchy, delicious deep-fried meal.

A trip to an ethnic grocery store may open up many new sources of delicious meals. Maize flour (masa harina), made from ground corn and used to make corn tortillas, works well. Risotto, a staple in Italian cooking, is a delicious alternative to pasta. Try flour substitutes in traditional recipes.

We found that despite owning a good pasta-making machine, commercial gluten-free pasta is much more sensible than homemade. So try one of the excellent gluten-free pastas available from your health or specialist food store and online retailers.

Remember, experimentation is part of the process, so don't get discouraged. When you start cooking, you may not get it right the first time. Keep trying until you do get it right.

Be creative. Vary ingredients and quantities and follow the recipes in this book for success. Bon appetit!

Chapter 2

Appetizers, Canapés and Salads

Piquant Artichoke and Spinach Dip

Makes 2 cups

1 10oz pack frozen chopped spinach, thawed
2 tablespoons olive oil
1 12oz jar artichoke hearts, drained and chopped
4oz cream cheese
8oz sour cream
1 teaspoon garlic powder
½ bunch spring onions, chopped
2 tablespoons fresh lemon juice
¼ teaspoon freshly grated nutmeg

For perfect party goodies, serve with gluten-free breads and crackers. You can make this in advance and then warm it up at the last minute.

1. Drain the thawed spinach, squeezing it with paper towels to remove excess liquid.

2. Heat the olive oil and add the spinach; cook until just soft, about 5 minutes.

3. Remove the pan from the heat and add the rest of the ingredients, stirring to mix. Serve warm or cold with celery or crackers.

The Artichoke Quandary

Some people absolutely adore artichokes that come in cans or jars; we like fresh or frozen. Cooking artichokes requires a bit more work, but even a busy person can cook ahead. After cooking baby artichokes, you can use them in a number of ways, simply removing the outside leaves.

Spicy Gorgonzola Dip with Red Pepper 'Spoons'

This is very flavourful – the more fresh herbs, the better.
Try using fresh chives, basil and oregano.

Makes 2 cups

6oz Gorgonzola cheese, at
   room temperature
4oz mayonnaise
4oz cream cheese, at room
   temperature
2oz roasted red peppers (from
   a jar is fine)
2 teaspoons fresh chopped
   herbs (such as oregano,
   basil and chives)
Salt, black pepper, and
   Tabasco sauce to taste
4 sweet red peppers

1. Put all but the raw red peppers into a food processor and blend until smooth. Scrape into a serving bowl.

2. Wash, core, and seed the red peppers, and then cut into chunks (these will be your 'spoons'). Place the red pepper spoons around the dip.

Exciting and Distinctive – and Healthy – Party Fare

Many of the party appetizers in this chapter are less fattening than plain old cheese and biscuits. They are definitely not boring, and many are full of healthy vitamins, minerals and phytochemicals. Bright red and yellow peppers are an excellent source of vitamin C.

Delicate Beef Flan

Serves 6

1 pint fresh beef stock
1 tablespoon gluten-free soy
    sauce
4 large eggs
8oz double or whipping
    cream
2 teaspoons dry sherry
baby salad leaves, to serve
6 leaves fresh sage, for
    garnish

*Serve this delightful custard over baby salad leaves
with red wine vinaigrette on the side.*

1. Heat the beef stock and let it boil until it is reduced to about two-thirds. Then add the soy sauce.

2. Preheat oven to 160°C/325°F/Gas 3.

3. Whisk the eggs, cream and sherry in a large bowl. When well blended, whisk in the stock.

4. Lightly oil six 4oz custard cups or ramekins. Divide the custard evenly between the cups. Place the cups in a large roasting tin with 2in-high sides. Set in the centre of the oven, and then add boiling water to the tin to come halfway up the sides of the cups.

5. Bake the custards until just set, about 30 minutes. Turn the custards out on to a bed of salad leaves. Decorate each with a fresh sage leaf and serve warm.

Light Gorgonzola and Ricotta Torte Appetizer

*This is light and delicious. You will find that it works best
in a springform cake tin. Serve warm or at room temperature.*

1. Preheat oven to 180°C/350°F/Gas 4.

2. Whizz the cheeses, oregano, lemon juice, zest, salt and pepper in a food processor until very smooth. Place in a bowl and fold in the beaten egg whites.

3. Oil the inside of a 10in springform cake tin. Add the cheese mixture, and bake for about 30 minutes or until slightly golden.

4. Sprinkle with hazelnuts. Cool slightly and serve in wedges.

The Ties that Bind

Gluten is the glue that holds breads, cakes and pastry together. When you substitute gluten-free flours for gluten-containing flours, you must use eggs or other stabilizers such as guar gum or xanthan gum to hold things together. However, though eggs work well for some recipes, forget about making gluten-free pasta – you need so much guar gum or xanthan gum that it gets slimy.

Serves 6

16oz fresh ricotta cheese
4oz Gorgonzola cheese,
    crumbled
1 teaspoon fresh oregano, or
    ¼ teaspoon dried
1 teaspoon fresh lemon juice
1 teaspoon freshly grated
    lemon zest
Salt and pepper to taste
3 egg whites, stiffly beaten
½ cup hazelnuts, chopped
    and toasted, for garnish

Savoury Chicken Spread

Makes 3 cups

2 cups cooked white or dark chicken

1 stalk celery, coarsely chopped

1–2 spring onions, white parts peeled

2 shallots, peeled

⅔ cup mayonnaise (not low fat)

1 teaspoon Madras curry powder

1 teaspoon Dijon mustard

1 teaspoon dried thyme leaves

½ teaspoon celery salt

Salt and freshly ground black pepper to taste

½ cup chopped fresh parsley

This is an excellent way to use leftover roast chicken or turkey.
It works nicely as a canapé, a stuffing for celery or a sandwich filling.

Place all ingredients in a food processor and whizz until coarsely blended. Scrape into an attractive bowl and chill until ready to serve. Good with toasted gluten-free baguette slices, crisps, or on lettuce as a first course. Possible garnishes include chopped chives, capers, sliced green or black olives, or baby pickled gherkins.

Hearty Mushrooms Stuffed with Spicy Beef

This recipe is wonderful on a chilly night. You can also serve larger portions of the mushrooms for lunch with a bowl of soup on the side.

1. To make the filling, place the beef, egg, chilli, garlic, onion, spices and salt in a food processor and mix thoroughly.

2. Carefully remove the stems from the mushrooms and pack them with the filling.

3. Preheat the oven to 160°C/325°F/Gas 3. Place the mushrooms in a baking dish and add enough water or white wine to cover the bottom of the dish.

4. Sprinkle with cheese and pine nuts. Bake for 35 minutes.

The Versatile Mushroom

Today, you can get really excellent commercially grown exotic mushrooms. Mushrooms can be called wild only if gathered in the wild. Try crimini mushrooms, which are small portobello mushrooms. Shiitakes have a very fine flavour, and oyster mushrooms are delicious. If you have no budgetary constraints, buy morels or chanterelles.

Serves 4

6oz lean ground beef
1 egg
2 tablespoons chilli sauce
1 clove garlic, chopped
½ cup chopped red onion
1in piece fresh ginger, peeled and chopped
⅛ teaspoon ground cinnamon
½ teaspoon crushed dried chillies, or to taste
½ teaspoon freshly ground black pepper
Salt to taste
8 very large fresh mushrooms
Water or white wine (enough to cover bottom of dish)
8 teaspoons freshly grated Parmesan cheese for topping
1oz pine nuts, for topping

Devilish Egg-Stuffed Celery

Makes 12 pieces

6 eggs, hard-boiled, cooled
    in water, cracked and
    peeled
2 tablespoons mayonnaise
6 drops Tabasco sauce
Freshly ground white pepper
    to taste
1 teaspoon celery salt
1 tablespoon Dijon mustard
2 tablespoons chopped onion
1 clove garlic, chopped
Salt to taste
2 tablespoons double cream
4 sticks celery, cut into thirds

For garnish:
    3 teaspoons salmon
    caviar, 3 teaspoons
    capers, 3 teaspoons green
    peppercorns, chopped
    fresh parsley, hot or sweet
    Hungarian paprika

*This is a different take on devilled eggs – you devil the whole egg.
The great thing about hard-boiled eggs is that they can be prepared
simply for kids or exquisitely for adults.*

Place all ingredients except the celery and the garnishes in a food processor and blend until smooth. Fill the celery sticks with the mixture and cover with foil or cling film and chill. Add garnishes just before serving.

An International Flavour

Chilli sauce and mayonnaise will add a Russian flavour to the eggs. Salmon caviar as a garnish will add a Scandinavian touch. Change the amount of heat and the herbs and you will have a different taste sensation. Experiment to find the flavour combinations you like best.

Traditional Chopped Chicken Liver

This traditional Jewish dish can be kosher or not, as the cook decides.
When the paté is garnished with bacon, it is definitely not kosher.

Makes 2 cups

1 sweet onion, finely chopped
3 tablespoons olive oil or
    rendered chicken fat
    (schmaltz)
1lb fresh chicken livers,
    trimmed
1 teaspoon salt and freshly
    ground black pepper
    to taste

1. Sauté the onion in 2 tablespoons oil and set aside on paper towels to drain.

2. Sauté the chicken livers in the same pan, adding an additional tablespoon of oil if necessary.

3. Either chop the livers by hand, mince or process them in a food processor, making sure they are not too fine.

4. Mix the onions, livers, and salt and pepper together and chill.

A Break with Tradition

The recipe given here is very basic; it can be changed with the addition of bacon, with a tablespoon of brandy, port or sherry. Crumbled hard-boiled eggs can be sprinkled on top for a different look. However it is served, this is a lovely hors d'oeuvre, fine on gluten-free crackers or thinly sliced toast rounds.

Sicilian Aubergine Rolls

Makes 10–15 rolls

1 large aubergine, peeled
Salt
½ cup olive oil
½ cup rice flour
1 cup ricotta cheese
¼ cup large green olives,
    pitted and chopped
¼ cup grated Parmesan
    cheese

*Make these in advance and warm them up when your guests come.
This also makes a great side dish for dinner.*

1. Cut the aubergine in very thin (⅛in) slices, using a mandolin. Salt the slices and stack them on a plate; put a weight on top and leave for half an hour to let the brown juices run out.

2. Pat the aubergine slices dry with paper towels.

3. Heat the oil to 150°C/300°F. Dip the slices in rice flour and fry until almost crisp, about 2 minutes per side.

4. Drain the slices and then place a spoonful of the cheese and some chopped olive on the end of each slice. Roll and secure with a cocktail stick.

5. Heat the oven to 150°C/300°F/Gas 2. Sprinkle the rolls with Parmesan cheese and bake for 8 minutes. Serve warm.

Aubergine Makes a Great Wrap

Aubergine can be sliced thinly lengthwise or crosswise and then fried, grilled or baked. Salting and stacking the slices under a weight will drain off the bitterness that some aubergines seem to harbour. Be sure to use a plate with steep sides or a bowl – some aubergines produce a lot of juice when salted.

Sweet Potato Crisps

Sweet potatoes are loaded with vitamin A and very delicious when fried and salted.

∾

1. Slice the potatoes thinly with a mandolin.

2. Heat the oil in a deep-fat fryer to 190°C/375°F.

3. Fry for about 3–4 minutes, depending on the thickness of the slices. When they are very crisp, remove from the oil and drain.

4. Add salt and pepper. Serve with a dip or eat plain.

Makes about 3 dozen

(You can substitute plantains for a taste of the Caribbean.)

2 large sweet potatoes, peeled
3 cups canola oil
Salt and pepper to taste

Mini Quiches

A wonderful cocktail party snack. You can vary the ingredients, using Cheddar cheese instead of Jarlsberg and chopped cooked bacon instead of ham.

∾

1. Preheat the oven to 160°C/325°F/Gas 3. Grease a mini-muffin tin and make up the pastry according to the instructions on the packet. Roll out thinly. With the rice-floured rim of a glass or a 2in biscuit cutter, cut the dough into 12 rounds and line the muffin cups with dough.

2. Mix the rest of the ingredients in a food processor.

3. Fill the cups three-quarters full with the cheese mixture.

4. Bake for about 10 minutes, or until the quiches are set. Leave to rest for 5 minutes. Carefully lift the Mini Quiches out of the tin. Serve warm.

Makes 12

1 package gluten-free pastry
2 eggs
½ cup grated Jarlsberg cheese
¼ cup chopped prosciutto or smoked ham
⅔ cup cream
⅛ teaspoon grated nutmeg
2 tablespoons chopped fresh chives
Freshly ground black pepper to taste

Bistro Lentil Salad

16oz red lentils or small
   French ones
2 cups chicken stock
Water, as needed
2 cloves garlic, peeled and
   bruised
2 whole cloves
4 slices smoked bacon
½ cup finely chopped red
   onion
1 sweet red pepper, roasted,
   peeled, and chopped
2 sticks celery, finely chopped
½ cup chopped fresh parsley
2 teaspoons dried oregano
1 teaspoon prepared Dijon
   mustard
2 tablespoons lemon juice
2 tablespoons red wine
   vinegar
⅔ cup extra virgin olive oil
Salt and freshly ground
   pepper to taste

*This is a favourite in French bistros and Greek tavernas. In either case,
the seasonings are only slightly different, in all cases delicious.*

1. Combine the lentils and stock and add water to cover. Add the garlic
   and cloves. Bring the lentils to the boil and reduce the heat to a simmer.
   Cook until tender, about 20 minutes. Drain and place in a large serving
   bowl. Remove the garlic and cloves.

2. Fry or grill the bacon until crisp, and drain on paper towels.

3. Mix the rest of the ingredients with the lentils and chill for 2–3 hours.
   Just before serving, heat for a few seconds in the microwave. Or serve
   well chilled with shredded lettuce. Garnish with crisp chopped bacon.

The Lovely Lentil

*Lentils are a staple in India, where many people need to be fed on little money.
You can become a gourmet on a budget, experimenting with many varieties of
lentils. Substitute them for pasta and use them in soups, stews, and salads.*

Golden Parmesan Crisps

It's important to use a block of fresh Parmesan cheese – the ready-grated stuff won't work as well because it's too fine and too dry.
Use the coarse grating blade of a food processor or box grater.

Makes 12 crisps

2 tablespoons unsalted butter (more if necessary)
12 heaped tablespoons coarsely grated fresh Parmesan cheese
Freshly ground black or cayenne pepper to taste

1. Heat the butter in a pan over a medium heat until it is foaming.

2. Drop the grated cheese by tablespoonfuls on to the butter, pressing down lightly with the back of the spoon to spread.

3. After about 2 minutes, turn and sauté until both sides are lightly golden brown. Add more butter if necessary.

4. Sprinkle with black pepper or cayenne, or both. Serve at once.

Classic Caesar Salad with Gluten-Free Croutons

Serves 4

1 head romaine lettuce
1 whole egg and 1 egg yolk,
    beaten
Freshly squeezed juice of
    ½ lemon
2 cloves garlic, chopped
1 teaspoon gluten-free
    English mustard
1in squeeze anchovy paste
    from a tube, or 2 canned
    anchovies, packed in oil,
    mashed
¾ cup extra virgin olive oil
Salt and freshly ground black
    pepper to taste
6 tablespoons freshly grated
    Parmesan cheese
24 Fresh Gluten-Free
    Croutons (see page 23)

Caesar salad has become unbelievably popular –
it is served with fried calamari, grilled chicken, prawns, fish and vegetables.

1. Wash and spin-dry the lettuce; then chop into bite-size pieces, wrap in a tea towel and place in the refrigerator to crisp.

2. Whisk together the egg, egg yolk, lemon juice, garlic, mustard, anchovy paste, and olive oil until very smooth. Add salt and pepper to taste. Add the lettuce and toss.

3. Sprinkle with Parmesan cheese and croutons, and serve.

Not That Caesar

According to the JNA Institute of Culinary Arts in Philadelphia, Caesar salad was originally created in 1924 by Caesar Cardini, an Italian restaurateur in Tijuana, Mexico. The salad is named after its creator – a chef – not Julius Caesar of the Roman Empire.

Fresh Gluten-Free Croutons

*These can be made in advance and stored in the refrigerator,
then crisped up at the last moment. Double the recipe for extras.*

Makes 24 croutons

½ cup olive oil
2 cloves garlic, chopped or
   put through a garlic press
4 slices gluten-free bread,
   thickly cut, crusts
   removed
Salt and pepper to taste

1. Preheat the grill to 180°C/350°F.

2. Mix the oil and garlic. Brush both sides of the bread with the garlicky oil. Sprinkle with salt and pepper to taste.

3. Cut each slice of bread into six, to make 24 cubes. Oil a baking sheet. Place the cubes on the sheet and grill until well browned on both sides.

4. Put the baking sheet on the bottom shelf of the oven. Turn off the oven and leave the croutons to dry for 20 minutes.

5. Store in an airtight container until ready to use.

For the Love of Garlic

Garlic will give you various degrees of potency depending on how you cut it. Finely chopped garlic, or that which has been put through a press, will be the strongest. When garlic is sliced, it is less strong, and when you leave the cloves whole, they are even milder.

Chapter 3

Breakfast and Brunch

Chestnut Flour Crêpes

Makes 12 crêpes

2 eggs
1 cup milk
½ teaspoon salt
½ cup chestnut flour
½ cup rice flour
2 teaspoons sugar (optional)
2 tablespoons butter, melted
    (plus extra for pan)

*Chestnut flour is sweet and nutty, making the most delicious
crêpes you can imagine. You can stuff them with fruit and
whipped cream, or with savoury fillings.*

1. Whizz the eggs, milk and salt in a food processor. With the motor on low, slowly add the flours, stopping occasionally to scrape down the sides of the bowl.

2. Add the sugar if you are making sweet crêpes with sweet filling; omit if you are going to fill them with savoury delights.

3. Pour in the melted butter and whizz until well blended. Pour about half a cupful of batter into a nonstick pancake pan to which you've added a dot of butter. Tilt the pan to spread the batter thinly.

4. Fry each crêpe on medium heat, turning, until browned on both sides; place on greaseproof paper and sprinkle with a little rice flour to prevent it from sticking.

5. When all the crêpes are done, you can fill them straight away or store them in the refrigerator or freezer for later use.

Using Nonstick Pans

Nonstick pans take all of the grief out of making crêpes. However, even if your pan is quite new, it's important to use a little butter for insurance and extra flavour. Keep the pan well buttered and you have an almost foolproof method for making perfect crêpes.

Chestnut Crêpes with Prosciutto and Peach Sauce

If you can't find mascarpone cheese, use cream cheese.
You can make the crêpes and sauce and fill the crêpes in advance.
Just heat everything up at the last moment.

Serves 4

2 tablespoons cornflour
¼ cup cold water
2 peaches, blanched, peeled, and sliced
Juice of ½ lemon
1 teaspoon hot red pepper sauce, or to taste
½ cup sugar
8 small Chestnut Flour Crêpes (see page 26)
Plenty of freshly ground black pepper
8 teaspoons mascarpone or cream cheese
8 paper-thin slices of prosciutto ham

1. Mix the cornflour with the cold water until very smooth. Place in a saucepan with the peaches, lemon juice, hot pepper sauce and sugar. You may need to add some more water if the peaches are not very juicy. Bring to the boil, stirring constantly, until very thick and syrupy. Taste for seasoning and add black pepper to taste.

2. Preheat the oven to 150°C/300°F/Gas 2.

3. Lay out the crêpes and spread each one with the cheese. Place a slice of ham over each and roll up. Lightly oil a shallow baking dish.

4. Arrange the rolls, seam side down, in the dish and bake for 10–15 minutes or until the crêpe rolls are hot. Serve with the peach syrup.

Buckwheat Pancakes with Sour Cream and Caviar

Serves 4–6

2 eggs
¾ cup buttermilk
½ cup rice flour
½ cup buckwheat flour
1 teaspoon sugar
1 teaspoon salt
1 tablespoon baking powder
½ teaspoon bicarbonate
   of soda
1 tablespoon butter, melted,
   plus 2 tablespoons for
   frying pancakes
1 cup sour cream
2oz salmon caviar

You can serve this 'Russian breakfast' at any time of day!
These pancakes should be made small, about 1½–2in in diameter.

1. Whisk the eggs and buttermilk together. Slowly beat in the rice flour, buckwheat flour, sugar, salt, baking powder, bicarbonate of soda and melted butter. You may have to add more milk to get a thick, creamy consistency.

2. Set the heat medium-high and butter a griddle or large frying pan. Drop large spoonfuls of batter on to the griddle. Turn the pancakes when you see bubbles coming up through the batter, about 3 minutes, and then cook for another 2 minutes, until golden. Serve with a dollop of sour cream and caviar.

Cooking with Buckwheat

Buckwheat has a flavour all its own. It's both nutty and slightly tart. Gluten-free buckwheat beer is available, or you can make it at home. The more you work with buckwheat, the more respect you will have for it. You can dress buckwheat pancakes with all kinds of sauces or toppings, such as mushroom, grilled vegetables and melted cheese.

Mushroom, Ham, and Cheese Crêpes

This filling is excellent for brunch, lunch or a light supper.
You can vary the herbs.

෨෦

1. Sauté the mushrooms in oil until softened. Add the sage leaves and salt and pepper. In a bowl, mix the mushrooms with the ricotta and egg.

2. Preheat the oven to 180°C/350°F/Gas 4.

3. Lay out the crêpes. Put a tablespoon of filling on one side of each. Roll up and put in an oiled baking dish. Cover with Basic White sauce and sprinkle with Parmesan cheese.

4. Bake for 20 minutes, and serve hot.

Makes 12 crêpes

12 Chestnut Flour Crêpes (see page 26) or Corn Crêpes (sugar omitted; see page 30)
6oz mushrooms, chopped
2 tablespoons olive oil
6 sage leaves, shredded
Salt and pepper to taste
½ cup ricotta cheese
1 egg, lightly beaten
1 recipe Basic White sauce (see page 200)
½ cup grated Parmesan cheese

Sweet and Spicy Apple-Cinnamon Crêpes

Just the aroma of this perfect weekend brunch dish will make you hungry.
It's going to get the kids out of bed too.

෨෦

1. Sauté the apples in butter for 20 minutes. Stir in cinnamon, cloves and sugar. Blend the cream cheese into the hot mixture.

2. Preheat the oven to 180°C/350°F/Gas 4.

3. Lay out the crêpes and place a spoonful of filling on each. Roll them up and place in an oiled baking dish.

4. Bake until hot, about 8–10 minutes. Serve with whipped cream or vanilla ice cream.

Makes 12 crêpes

2 large tart apples, such as Granny Smith, peeled, cored and chopped
1 tablespoon butter
1 teaspoon cinnamon
¼ teaspoon ground cloves
2 tablespoons brown sugar, or to taste
4oz cream cheese, at room temperature
12 Chestnut Flour Crêpes (see page 26), with sugar
Whipped cream or ice cream

Corn Crêpes

2 eggs
1 cup milk or buttermilk
1 teaspoon salt or to taste
1 cup maize flour (masa harina)
2 teaspoons sugar (optional)
2 tablespoons butter, melted
Vegetable oil for frying crêpes

As with the Chestnut Flour Crêpes (see page 26), you can make these in advance and store them in the refrigerator or freezer.

1. Place the eggs, milk and salt in a food processor and whizz until smooth. With the motor on low, slowly add the flour and spoon in the sugar if you are making sweet crêpes. Scrape down the sides of the bowl often. Add the melted butter.

2. Heat a nonstick pan over medium heat and add a spoonful of vegetable oil. Pour in the batter to make the first crêpe. Tilt the pan to spread the batter evenly.

3. As they are done, place the crêpes on sheets of greaseproof paper that have been dusted with extra maize flour.

4. To store, place in a plastic bag in the refrigerator or freezer. You can stuff these crêpes with salsa, cheese and sour cream, or with mashed fruit such as strawberries.

Storing Crêpes

If you are not using the crêpes immediately, simply put a little maize flour on sheets of greaseproof paper and stack them individually. Then put the whole thing in a plastic bag and store.

Corn Crêpes with Eggs, Cheese and Salsa

These Mexican-style crêpes make a fantastic brunch!

༄

1. Place the crêpes on oiled baking sheets. Put a slice of cheese on each crêpe. Place one egg on each piece of cheese. Spoon a bit of salsa on top of each egg.

2. Preheat the grill to 200°C/400°F. Sprinkle the crêpes with Parmesan cheese and grill for about 5 minutes, until the cheese is hot and starting to melt.

3. You can put the sliced cheese on top of the eggs if you wish, and serve the salsa on the side.

Makes 12 crêpes

1 recipe Corn Crêpes (see page 30)
12 thin slices Monterey jack or Cheddar cheese
12 eggs, poached or fried
12 teaspoons salsa
12 teaspoons grated Parmesan cheese

Corn Crêpes with Salmon and Cream Cheese

Serves 4

12 Corn Crêpes (see page 30)
4oz cream cheese, at room
    temperature
4oz sliced smoked salmon
½ sweet onion, thinly sliced
Condiments such as
    horseradish, chopped
    chives, mustard

Love the taste of smoked salmon and cream cheese? These crêpes will hit the spot. You can substitute unsweetened whipped cream for the cream cheese.

1. Toast the crêpes on a baking sheet under the grill at 180°C/350°F for about 5 minutes. Spread with cream cheese.

2. Place the sliced salmon over the cheese and let people help themselves to onion slices and condiments.

Corn Is a Crucial Food

Cornmeal is an ancient grain, first raised in South and Central America. It made its way north as seeds were passed by native tribes. By the time the Pilgrim Fathers got to Massachusetts, corn was a staple in North America. It's hardy, sustaining and a 'hot' food, warming the body. Without corn, or maize, supplied by sympathetic Indians, the first European settlers in North America would not have survived.

Corn Crêpes with Ricotta and Herb Filling

*Try a variety of herbs in the filling, such as
fresh basil, sage, oregano or chopped rosemary.*

1. In a food processor, whizz the ricotta cheese, eggs, Parmesan cheese, salt, pepper and basil.

2. Preheat the oven to 160°C/325°F/Gas 3. Lay the crêpes out and place a tablespoon of filling on the end of each one. Roll them up and arrange them in a greased baking dish.

3. Pour the sauce over the crêpes. Sprinkle with grated cheese. Bake for 25 minutes. Serve hot.

Makes 12 crêpes

1½ cups ricotta cheese
2 eggs
¼ cup finely grated Parmesan cheese
Salt and freshly ground black pepper, to taste
¼ cup basil leaves (or your favourite herbs)
1 recipe Corn Crêpes (see page 30)
1 recipe Basic White sauce (see page 200)
1 cup grated Cheddar cheese

Herbs and Spices

People often confuse herbs with spices. Herbs are green and are the leaves of plants – the only herb (in Western cooking) that is a flower is lavender. Frequently used herbs include parsley, basil, oregano, thyme, rosemary, coriander and mint. Spices are roots, tubers, barks or berries. These include pepper, cinnamon, nutmeg, allspice, cumin, turmeric, ginger, cardamom and coriander seed.

Blueberry or Strawberry Griddle Cakes

Fruit on, or inside, griddle cakes is classic, healthy and delicious.

Makes 12 griddle cakes

½ pint blueberries or
    strawberries
1 tablespoon sugar
1 teaspoon orange zest
1 recipe Basic Griddle Cakes
    batter (see page 35)

1. In a bowl, mix the fruit, sugar and orange zest. Mash with a potato masher or pestle.

2. Heat a griddle or large frying pan to medium. Add butter. Pour on spoonfuls of batter to fit comfortably and spoon some berries on top of each cake.

3. Turn when bubbles rise to the top of the cakes, and brown the other side. You will get some caramelization from the sugar and fruit – it's delicious. Top with more berries and whipped cream.

Freezing Fruit in Its Prime

There's nothing like blueberry pie in January, and we're not talking about the fruit that comes all ready and loaded with sugar syrup in a can. When fresh blueberries are available, just rinse them and dry on paper towels. Place the berries on a baking sheet in the freezer for half an hour and then put them in a plastic bag for future use.

Basic Griddle Cakes

For a lighter griddle cake, separate the eggs and beat the whites stiffly.
These are great with mashed fresh peaches,
strawberries and/or blueberries.

ᕯᕐᕐ

1. In the bowl of a food processor, whizz all the liquid ingredients. Slowly add the baking powder and flour.

2. Heat a griddle or large frying pan to medium. Drop a teaspoon of butter on it and when the butter sizzles, start pouring on the batter to make cakes about 2in in diameter.

3. When bubbles come to the top, turn the griddle cakes and continue to cook until golden brown. Place on a plate in a warm oven to keep warm while you make the others.

Flour Substitutions

Try substituting rice or potato flour in some recipes, and chickpea flour also makes excellent savoury pancakes. You have so many choices – it's fun to exercise them.

Makes 16 griddle cakes

½ cup milk
2 eggs
1½ tablespoons butter, melted
1 tablespoon baking powder
1 cup rice flour (or substitute maize, chickpea or tapioca flour)
Extra butter for cooking

Banana Nut Griddle Cakes

Serves 4

1 banana
Extra butter for cooking
1 recipe Basic Griddle Cakes
 batter (see page 35)
1 cup coarsely chopped
 walnuts
1 cup double cream whipped
 with 1 tablespoon sugar

The bananas can be either sliced on to the cakes or mashed and incorporated into the batter.

1. Whizz the banana in a food processor until smooth.

2. Heat a large frying pan or griddle over medium heat. Add butter and pour large spoonfuls of the batter. Sprinkle nuts on top of each cake.

3. Turn when the cakes begin to bubble on top. Place on a warm platter. Serve with freshly whipped cream.

Luscious Ricotta Griddle Cakes

Makes 12 griddle cakes

1 cup ricotta cheese
2 whole eggs plus 1 egg yolk
⅓ cup plus 1 tablespoon rice
 or tapioca flour
1 teaspoon vanilla
1 teaspoon bicarbonate
 of soda
½ teaspoon salt
⅛ teaspoon nutmeg
⅛ teaspoon cinnamon
2 tablespoons unsalted
 butter, melted, plus extra
 for cooking

Preparing the batter in your blender makes it velvety smooth. You can serve with fruit, or dress with a berry coulis. The ricotta adds protein.

1. Whizz the ingredients in a blender, adding them in the order given, finishing with the melted butter.

2. Set a griddle or large frying pan over medium heat and melt a liberal amount of butter on it. When the butter foams, start dropping quarter cupfuls of batter on the griddle.

3. After 4 minutes, turn the cakes and cook the other side. Stack on a platter in a low oven to keep warm until ready to serve. Serve with fruit, syrup or a fruit coulis.

Southern Fried Green or Yellow Tomatoes

Use tomatoes that are very firm. They usually aren't very large, so count on two per person. Serve with thick slices of country ham or Irish bacon.

෨

1. Spread the flour mixed with salt and pepper on one sheet of greaseproof paper and the cornmeal on another. Place the whisked eggs in a bowl between the two.

2. Dip the tomato slices first in the flour, then in the egg, and coat them with cornmeal.

3. Heat ½in of oil in a frying pan to 180°C/350°F. Slide the tomato slices in and fry for 4 minutes or until well browned. Turn and finish frying.

4. Drain on paper towels. Serve as a side dish with eggs and bacon. As an extra fillip, you can add a dollop of sour cream to each tomato slice.

Serves 4

1 cup maize flour (masa harina)
Coarsely ground black pepper to taste
1 cup cornmeal
2 whole eggs whisked in a large flat soup bowl
8 green or yellow tomatoes, cores trimmed, cut in ⅓in slices
Oil for frying
1 teaspoon salt

Italian Ricotta and Chestnut Fritters

This is a traditional Italian recipe. These fritters are a wonderful side dish for brunch with bacon or ham, and they're easy to make.

෨

1. Beat the eggs and sugar until thick. Slowly add the rest of the ingredients except the vegetable oil and the icing sugar. Cover the bowl and leave to stand for 1 hour.

2. Heat 2in of oil over a medium-high heat to 190°C/375°F. Drop the batter by tablespoonfuls into the oil. Do not overfill the pan. Fry for about 2 minutes, turning as they brown.

3. Drain on brown paper or paper towels and dust with icing sugar.

Serves 4

2 eggs
½ cup sugar
1 teaspoon vanilla extract
1 teaspoon bicarbonate of soda
1 cup ricotta cheese
½ cup chestnut flour
½ cup rice flour
Vegetable oil for frying
Icing sugar to dust fritters

Shirred Eggs with Crumbled Cheddar Topping

12 extra large eggs
Salt and pepper to taste
4 tablespoons butter
¾ cup grated Cheddar cheese

*These are just plain cute and so appealing. For an extra touch,
you can place a thin slice of tomato in the bottom of each ramekin.*

1. Preheat the oven to 180°C/350°F/Gas 4. Lightly oil 12 small ramekins or 6 larger ones. Place the ramekins on a baking sheet. Break 1 egg into each small ramekin or 2 eggs into each large one.

2. Sprinkle the eggs with salt and pepper and dot with butter.

3. Sprinkle with grated Cheddar and bake for 8–12 minutes until the egg whites are set. Serve immediately.

An Elegant Touch

If you are having a crowd of people to brunch, place ramekins on a baking sheet and bake for 10 minutes. Then serve with a big bowl of fruit on the side. You can use glass custard cups, but individual ramekins made of white porcelain are more elegant.

Cheese Torte with Serrano Ham and Parmesan

If you can't find sweet-tasting Serrano ham, substitute prosciutto or another dry-cured raw ham.

1. Sauté the shallots in butter and place in a greased flan dish. Preheat the oven to 160°C/325°F/Gas 3.

2. Beat the eggs and add the rest of the ingredients, beating all the time. Pour into the prepared dish and bake for 35 minutes, or until set and golden. Cut into wedges and serve.

Serves 6

2 shallots, peeled and chopped
2 tablespoons butter
3 eggs
1lb curd cheese
½ cup Parmesan cheese, grated
¼ cup Serrano or prosciutto ham, finely chopped
4 tablespoons butter, melted
1 teaspoon dried oregano
⅛ teaspoon nutmeg
Salt and pepper to taste

Spicy Egg-and-Cheese-Stuffed Tomatoes

Serves 4

8 medium tomatoes
2 cloves garlic, chopped or
    put through a garlic press
4 tablespoons butter
1 teaspoon salt
1 teaspoon black pepper
1 teaspoon cayenne pepper
1 teaspoon dried oregano
1 teaspoon ground cumin
8 eggs
½ cup grated Cheddar cheese
8 teaspoons gluten-free
    cornbread crumbs

This is a fine way to use up the end-of-summer tomatoes in your garden.

1. Cut the tops off the tomatoes, core, and using a melon baller, scoop out the seeds and pulp. Place the tomatoes on a baking sheet covered with baking parchment.

2. Preheat the oven to 180°C/350°F/Gas 4.

3. Sauté the garlic in the butter. While it's cooking, mix together the salt, black pepper, cayenne pepper, oregano and cumin in a small bowl.

4. Rub the insides of the tomatoes with half the spice mixture. Spoon the butter and garlic mixture into the tomatoes. Sprinkle with half the remaining spice mixture, saving a little for the eggs.

5. Break an egg into each tomato. Sprinkle with the rest of the spice mixture. Scatter the cheese over the eggs, then sprinkle 1 teaspoon cornbread crumbs over each tomato. Bake for 20 minutes. The tomatoes should still be firm, the eggs soft, the cheese melted and the breadcrumbs browned.

Priceless Heirlooms

There are good tomatoes in the supermarket and good tomatoes in cans, but the best tomatoes are homegrown. Recently there has been a trend toward growing ancient varieties of tomato. These 'heirlooms', as they are called, have more flavour, sweetness paired with acidity, then ordinary tomatoes do. You can buy the seeds and grow them yourself, and some farmers' markets have them too.

Ham and Asparagus Rolls with Cheese

This is excellent for a cold morning. It's tasty enough to get things going, and hearty enough to stay with you for a morning of skiing or tobogganing outdoors.

෨෧

1. Preheat the oven to 180°C/350°F/Gas 4. Lay out the slices of ham. Place a slice of cheese and then an asparagus spear on each ham slice. Roll up and secure with cocktail sticks if necessary.

2. Place the rolls in a lightly oiled glass baking dish. Pour the cheese sauce over the top.

3. Bake for 25 minutes or until lightly browned on top and heated through. Serve hot.

Serves 6

1lb fresh asparagus, trimmed and cooked, or 14oz can asparagus spears
½lb smoked ham, thinly sliced
½lb processed cheese, thinly sliced
1 recipe Creamy Cheddar Sauce with Ham and Sherry (see page 201)

Pesto with Basil and Mint

Serves 4

½ cup pine nuts, toasted
2 cloves garlic, peeled
4 cups, packed, fresh basil
    leaves
½ cup, packed, fresh mint
    leaves
1 cup olive oil
1 cup grated Parmesan
    cheese
Salt and pepper to taste

*This variation on an old classic is delicious with hard-boiled or poached
eggs, over pasta, or as a condiment with cold meat or poultry.
It's very good over sliced cold chicken.*

Put all the ingredients in a blender and whizz until smooth. Serve as a
side dish over pasta or with cold meat.

Sweet and Hot!

*Mixing sweet things with a bit of spicy heat will make an intriguing flavour
combo. Think of all the salsas that mix fruit with jalapeño (or even hotter)
chilli peppers – they are wonderful. Try different kinds of fruit sauces, adding
a trace of peppery heat each time, until you find several you really like to serve.
Experiment with mangos, pineapple, nectarines, apricots and whatever else is
in season.*

Chapter 4

Casseroles and Entrées

Beef Stroganoff

Serves 6

2 tablespoons olive oil

4 shallots, peeled and
    chopped

8oz tiny button mushrooms,
    stems removed

2 garlic cloves, chopped

2 tablespoons tapioca flour
    plus ¼ cup for coating the
    meat

1 teaspoon dried mustard

Salt and pepper to taste

1½ cups beef stock

1 cup red wine

1 teaspoon Worcestershire
    sauce

2lb beef fillet, cut into bite-
    sized cubes

2 tablespoons unsalted butter

2 tablespoons snipped fresh
    dill

1 cup sour cream or crème
    fraîche

*This is an elegant, historic recipe, named after the Russian
general who is said to have invented it. You can serve it with
potato pancakes on the side, or with wild rice.*

1. In a large sauté pan, heat the oil over medium heat and add the shallots, mushrooms and garlic. Cook for 5 minutes to soften. Add the 2 table-spoons of flour, mustard, salt and pepper, stirring to blend.

2. Mix in the beef stock and heat, stirring, until it thickens. Stir in the wine and Worcestershire sauce and bring to the boil. Turn off the heat.

3. On a large piece of greaseproof paper, roll the beef in flour. Heat the unsalted butter in a separate pan. Sear the beef in the butter. Spoon the beef into the mushroom sauce, add the dill and stir to blend. Simmer for 10–15 minutes; the beef should be medium-rare.

4. Just before serving, add the sour cream. Spoon over a bed of wild rice or serve with potato pancakes on the side.

Why Not to Wash Mushrooms

Mushrooms are grown in a safe and sanitary medium, often horse manure that has been treated with thermophilic bacteria. This kills any germs by naturally heating the growing medium to a very high temperature. Washing mushrooms makes them mushy because they absorb the water. Please don't peel them, either – just brush any compost off them.

Las Chalupas with Crêpe-atillas

You can make these delightful crêpes in advance, then either refrigerate or freeze them. Make them for a casual party for your family or for your teenage children and their friends.

1. Whizz the eggs, milk or water, salt, pepper and flour in the blender until smooth, stopping once to scrape down the sides of the goblet. Leave the batter to rest for 30 minutes or more. The flour may soak up extra liquid and the batter should be very thin. If it is too thick, add extra milk.

2. Heat the oil or melt the butter in a nonstick pan and fry eight 6in crêpes until light golden on both sides. Set aside on greaseproof paper that you have sprinkled with flour.

3. Sauté the beef and onion, gradually adding the rest of the ingredients, except the toppings, and stirring until well blended.

4. Place the crêpes on plates and let your guests add their favourite toppings.

Serves 4

2 eggs
1½ cups milk or water
½ teaspoon salt or seasoned salt (or to taste)
¼ teaspoon pepper (or to taste)
1 cup maize flour (masa harina)
Butter or cooking oil for frying
1lb ground beef
1 small onion, chopped
2 pickled jalapeños, chopped, and 2 tablespoons of their juice
1 teaspoon garlic powder
1 cup salsa
1 tablespoon chilli powder
Salt and black pepper to taste

Toppings:
2 cups grated Monterey jack cheese, 2 cups grated Cheddar cheese, shredded iceberg or romaine lettuce, chopped tomato, chopped black or green olives, Guacamole (see page 251), 1 cup sour cream

Chestnut Cannelloni with Sage, Mushrooms and Wine Sauce

Serves 6

2 eggs
1 teaspoon salt
Freshly ground white pepper
    to taste
1 cup milk
1 cup chestnut flour
Vegetable oil or unsalted
    butter for cooking
1 cup ricotta cheese
2 eggs
¼ teaspoon nutmeg
½ cup smoked ham, thinly
    sliced and shredded
½ cup chopped fresh
    flat-leaf parsley
½ cup freshly grated
    Parmesan cheese
2 shallots, chopped
2 cups mushrooms, sliced
½ cup olive oil
1 tablespoon cornflour
1 cup dry white wine
½ cup chicken stock
10 fresh sage leaves, chopped
Salt and pepper to taste
Grated Parmesan cheese for
    the topping

The number of cannelloni you make depends not on the recipe but on how large and thick you make them. Plan on two stuffed tubes per person.

1. Put the eggs, salt, pepper, milk and flour into a blender or food processor and whizz until smooth.

2. Heat plenty of oil or butter in a nonstick pan over medium heat. Pour enough batter into the hot pan to coat the base, moving the pan around in circles to spread the batter evenly.

3. Fry for a few minutes on each side; don't over- or undercook or the pasta will tear. Stack on sheets of greaseproof paper and store in a plastic bag in the refrigerator until ready to use (if making it in advance).

4. Preheat the oven to 180°C/350°F/Gas 4.

5. Mix the ricotta, eggs, nutmeg, ham, parsley and Parmesan in a bowl and, laying out the cannelloni, spread a tablespoon across one edge. Carefully roll the pasta into a tube and place in a buttered baking dish.

6. Sauté the shallots and mushrooms in the olive oil. Add the cornflour and stir until thickened. Blend in the wine and stock, the sage, salt and pepper. Pour over the cannelloni and sprinkle with grated Parmesan cheese. Bake for 30 minutes.

Variation on a Theme

This is wonderfully delicious and easy to make in advance, storing the pasta for future use. A fine variation is to add some spinach to the ricotta stuffing. You can also substitute prosciutto for regular ham.

Savoury Rice and Sausage

This is so easy and really great for any time when you are really busy. Kids love it and grown-ups do too.

෯෨

1. In a large ovenproof frying pan or casserole dish, brown the sausage pieces, onion and garlic. If the sausage is very lean, add a little olive oil to prevent the food from sticking.

2. Stir in the rice and toss with the sausage and vegetables. Add the stock and rosemary and cover. Cook on very low heat or place in the oven at 160°C/325°F/Gas 3 for 45 minutes to 1 hour, depending on the type of rice you are using.

3. Just before serving, sprinkle the top with Parmesan cheese and brown under the grill. Add the chopped parsley and serve.

The Old-Fashioned Ways

Once seasoned, a heavy black wrought-iron frying pan will last for generations. In fact, they never wear out. And being of such thick metal, they distribute heat evenly. Seasoning the pan requires leaving just a skim of oil on a warm pan overnight. Then, don't overuse detergent. Pass your pans on to your grandchildren, especially if yours came from your grandmother.

Serves 4–6

1lb sausages, cut into 1in pieces
1 medium onion, finely chopped
2 cloves garlic, chopped
1 cup rice
2¾ cups chicken stock
1 teaspoon dried rosemary, or 1 tablespoon fresh rosemary
Grated Parmesan cheese and chopped fresh parsley to garnish

Scalloped Potatoes with Leeks and Country Ham

*This is a great brunch or supper dish.
It's filling and delicious, especially good on a cold day or nippy evening.*

Serves 6

1½ cups grated Parmesan
   cheese
1 cup coarsely grated Fontina
   cheese
½ cup maize flour (masa
   harina)
Salt and freshly ground black
   pepper to taste
6 large waxy potatoes, peeled
   and sliced thinly
4 leeks, white parts only,
   thinly sliced crosswise
1lb thickly sliced ham, diced
3 cups milk
4 tablespoons butter

1. Butter a baking dish. Preheat the oven to 180°C/350°F/Gas 4.

2. Mix together the cheeses, maize flour, salt and pepper.

3. Place a layer of potatoes in the baking dish, then one of leeks, and dab with bits of ham. Sprinkle with the mixture of cheeses, maize flour and spices. Repeat until you get to the top of the baking dish. Add the milk, sprinkle with the remaining cheese mixture and dot with butter.

4. Bake for about 90 minutes. The top should be brown and crispy, the inside soft and creamy.

Tuscan Bean, Tomato and Parmesan Casserole

*When you are trying to whip up something satisfying,
warming, and delicious for a cold and stormy night, this is it!*

Serves 4–6

4 slices bacon
¼ cup olive oil
4 cloves garlic, chopped
    coarsely
1 medium onion, peeled and
    chopped coarsely
½ fresh fennel bulb, coarsely
    chopped
1 tablespoon rice flour
2 cans cannellini beans,
    drained and rinsed
16oz tomatoes, chopped
    (canned is fine)
1 medium courgette,
    chopped
1 tablespoon chopped fresh
    basil
1 teaspoon dried oregano
½ cup fresh flat-leaf parsley,
    chopped
1 teaspoon dried chilli flakes,
    or to taste
1 teaspoon salt, or to taste
½ cup freshly grated
    Parmesan cheese
2 tablespoons unsalted
    butter, cut into
    small pieces

1. Fry the bacon until almost crisp. Place on paper towels to drain. Remove all but 1 teaspoon of bacon fat from the frying pan. Add the oil, garlic, onion and fennel. Sauté over a low heat for 10 minutes, or until softened but not browned.

2. Preheat the oven to 180°C/350°F/Gas 4. Blend the flour into the mixture and cook for 3 minutes, blending well.

3. Add the beans, tomatoes, and courgette. Mix well and pour into a casserole dish. Add the herbs, chilli flakes and salt. Stir in the reserved chopped bacon.

4. Sprinkle Parmesan cheese and butter over the top and bake for 25 minutes, or until the cheese is lightly browned.

Eat More Beans

There are more varieties of legumes than it's possible to list here. They are delicious and loaded with protein, vitamins, minerals and fibre. If a culture, or a household, needs to stretch its food supply, beans are the answer. They come in red and pink, green and orange, black and white, speckled or solid. Some have black eyes and others look like cranberries. Beans – legumes – are available in many sizes and shapes, from tiny peas to big kidney beans.

Spaghetti Squash with Creamy Vodka and Prawn Sauce

Serves 6

1 large (4–5lb) spaghetti squash, cooked
2 chopped shallots
2 tablespoons olive oil
1 tablespoon butter
1 tablespoon cornflour
½ cup vodka
2 14oz cans chopped tomatoes
1 cup double cream
1½lb raw prawns, peeled and deveined
Salt and plenty of freshly ground pepper to taste
½ cup each chopped fresh parsley and basil
¼ cup prosciutto ham, chopped, for garnish

The squash can be prepared a day in advance. Its fresh taste lends itself to many sauces, from a tomatoey marinara to a meaty Bolognese.

1. Place the cooked squash in a large bowl and keep warm while you make the sauce.

2. Sauté the chopped shallots in a mixture of oil and butter. When soft, add the cornflour. Cook and stir over a low heat until well blended, then add the vodka and tomatoes.

3. Cover and simmer gently for 20 minutes.

4. Stir in the cream and heat slowly, then add the prawns. Do not boil after the cream has been added. When the prawns turn pink, pour over the spaghetti squash, and add salt and pepper to taste. Garnish with parsley, basil and prosciutto.

Parmesan Cheese

Always grate Parmesan cheese yourself as you need it. Buy it in blocks and keep well wrapped in the refrigerator. Try using a box grater for a coarse cheese with lots of body.

Hollandaise Sauce

If the sauce gets too hot, it will curdle. To rescue it, pour it back into the blender and add a tablespoon of boiling water, then blitz it for 30 seconds.

Makes 1½ cups

½lb unsalted butter
Juice of 1 lemon
2 egg yolks plus 1 whole egg
⅛ teaspoon cayenne pepper
Salt and freshly ground black pepper to taste

1. Melt the butter in a saucepan. Meanwhile, place the lemon juice, egg yolks, whole egg and cayenne in the goblet of a blender.

2. When the butter has melted, reduce the heat to very low. Very slowly pour the melted butter into the blender, set on low.

3. Return the sauce to the pan in which you heated the butter and stir constantly until thickened. Remove from the heat; add salt and pepper. Serve immediately.

Chicken Divan

This is so exquisite that you won't miss potatoes, pastry or pasta.
It stands alone as a one-dish meal.

Serves 6

1lb broccoli, divided into florets, cooked, and drained
3lb chicken breasts, boneless and skinless, cut into strips
1 cup maize flour (masa harina)
Salt and freshly ground black pepper to taste
½ cup olive oil, or more as needed
1½ cups Hollandaise Sauce (see page 51)
2 tablespoons grated Parmesan cheese
Sprinkle of paprika (optional)

1. Make sure the cooked broccoli is well drained. You can cook it in advance and place it in the refrigerator on paper towels.

2. Roll the chicken in the flour and sprinkle with salt and pepper. Preheat the oven to 180°C/350°F/Gas 4.

3. Heat the olive oil in a sauté pan. Sauté the chicken for 5 minutes on each side until golden brown, adding more oil if the pan gets dry.

4. Butter a 4-pint casserole. Place the broccoli in the bottom and spoon some Hollandaise over the top. Arrange the chicken over the broccoli and pour on the rest of the sauce. Sprinkle with grated Parmesan cheese and paprika. Bake for 30 minutes.

Turkey and Fruit

Vary the flavours in this dish by adding fresh sage or fresh parsley.
You can also substitute a variety of mushrooms for the fruit.

Serves 4

2 tablespoons butter
½ cup chopped sweet onion
2 sticks celery, chopped
2 tart apples, peeled, cored
   and chopped
2 ripe pears, peeled, cored
   and chopped
½ cup dried cranberries
1 teaspoon dried thyme
   leaves
2 teaspoons dried rosemary
   spikes, crumbled
1¼lb sliced fresh turkey breast
   or thigh
Salt and pepper to taste
½ cup apple cider
½ cup chicken stock
1½ cups gluten-free
   cornbread crumbs

1. Melt the butter and add the onion and celery. Sauté until soft, about 10 minutes, over a low heat. Add the fruit and seasonings. Cook until just tender, about 5 more minutes.

2. Preheat the oven to 180°C/350°F/Gas 4.

3. Butter a baking dish. Sprinkle the turkey with salt and pepper and place it in the dish. Cover it with the fruit mixture.

4. Add the cider and stock. Sprinkle the top with cornbread crumbs and moisten with juice. Bake for 45 minutes.

Serving Suggestion – Serve with Rice

More varieties of rice are now on the market. It used to be just long and short grain. Today, you can buy Arborio rice from Italy and basmati rice, the staple of the Indian and Chinese diets. You can also buy purple rice, brown rice and sticky rice. Arborio and basmati rices are short grained and stubby. They make a lot more 'cream' than other varieties. Try them all and you will find favourites. Basmati and Arborio varieties are wonderful in risotto, baked rice and rice pudding.

Moroccan Aubergine and Lamb Casserole

With this recipe, you don't have to worry about a top crust or thickening. If you like it thick, just add a bit of cornflour or rice flour.

Serves 4

2 large aubergines, peeled
    and cut vertically into
    long, thin slices
Table salt
1 red onion, peeled and diced
4 cloves garlic, peeled and
    chopped
¼ cup olive oil, plus extra for
    sautéing
1¼lb very lean ground lamb
¼ teaspoon cinnamon
½ teaspoon ground coriander
    seeds
Juice of 1 lemon
½ cup sultanas
½ cup dried apricots,
    chopped
1 cup chopped tomatoes,
    with their juice
10 fresh mint leaves, torn into
    small pieces
Salt and pepper to taste
Hot paprika or cayenne to
    taste

1. Slice the aubergine and stack it with plenty of salt between the layers. Leave it to rest while you prepare the filling.

2. Sauté the onion and garlic in a tablespoon of olive oil. Add the lamb when the vegetables are soft.

3. Add the rest of the ingredients and cook, stirring, until well blended. The apricots will absorb much of the liquid. If still very liquid, sprinkle with a teaspoon of cornflour. Cover and simmer for 15 minutes.

4. Preheat the oven to 180°C/350°F/Gas 4.

5. Drain any liquid from the aubergine and arrange a single layer in a well-oiled 11 x 13in baking dish. Add some of the lamb mixture, distributing it evenly. Keep making layers until you have one final layer of aubergine. Sprinkle with extra oil and bake for 45 minutes. Serve in wedges. The traditional accompaniment is rice.

Aubergines in Lavender, Purple and White

Aubergines come in a number of sizes, shapes and colours – they all taste pretty much the same. The larger ones may have bitter seeds, and an old method of sweetening them up is to peel and cut them paper-thin, salt the slices on each side and stack them on a plate, under a weight. Then, a lot of brown juice comes out, and the slices are sweet.

Veal Loaf with Red Peppers and Gorgonzola

*The water bath (or bain-marie) technique used here will make
this tender meat loaf almost custard-like.*

৩৩

1. Preheat the oven to 160°C/325°F/Gas 3. Whizz the veal, onion, garlic, eggs, breadcrumbs, oregano, salt, pepper and chilli sauce in a food processor until smooth.

2. Grease a standard 9 x 5in loaf tin. Pour half the mixture into the tin. Spread a layer of roasted red peppers on top and scatter the crumbled Gorgonzola over that. Add the rest of the veal mixture. Sprinkle with Parmesan cheese.

3. Place the loaf tin inside a large roasting tin, and add enough boiling water to come halfway up the sides of the loaf tin. Place in the oven and bake for 1 hour.

Basil

Basil is a versatile herb – raw or cooked, dry or fresh, it adds immeasurably to many main dishes, sauces, salads and soups. In the old Italian lore, it was considered bad luck to chop basil with a knife – one was told to tear it carefully. The edges from tearing are not so clean and sharp, so perhaps they let more aroma and flavour out of the leaves. Basil also comes in a number of different varieties with different flavours. The standard Italian basil is fine for everything. At the end of the summer, pick all the basil you have grown, tie it in bunches and let them dry. They will last all winter.

Serves 4–6

1½lb ground veal
1 small onion
2 cloves garlic
2 eggs
*1 cup gluten-free
    breadcrumbs*
1 tablespoon oregano
Salt and pepper to taste
½ cup gluten-free chilli sauce
*2 roasted red peppers, packed
    in olive oil*
*3oz Gorgonzola cheese,
    crumbled*
*2 tablespoons grated
    Parmesan cheese*

Courgettes with Seafood, Tomato and Bacon

Serves 6

6 large courgettes
1 small onion, peeled and
    chopped
2 cloves garlic, peeled and
    chopped
1 serrano or other hot chilli,
    cored, seeded, and
    chopped
2 tablespoons butter or olive
    oil
1 cup cooked rice
1 cup chopped tomatoes
1lb crabmeat
2 tablespoons freshly
    squeezed lemon juice
2 eggs
1 tablespoon dried oregano
    leaves or 2 tablespoons
    fresh oregano
Salt and pepper to taste
6 rashers of streaky bacon for
    garnish

*This recipe can use up small marrows,
but it's better with large courgettes, about 10in long.*

1. Cut the top quarter off the courgettes, lengthwise. Hollow out the courgettes with a melon baller or a teaspoon; reserve the pulp.

2. Sauté the onion, garlic, pepper, and courgette pulp in the butter until soft. Add all the remaining ingredients except the bacon.

3. Preheat the oven to 180°C/350°F/Gas 4.

4. Divide the filling among the courgette boats. Lay a rasher of bacon on top of each stuffed courgette. Place in an oiled baking dish. Bake until the "boats" are hot and the bacon is brown and crisp. Serve hot or at room temperature.

Stuffed Vegetables

There are many vegetables you can successfully stuff with lots of different delicious ingredients. Chopped meat, prawns, fish and crabmeat make wonderful stuffings. A baked clam-stuffed mushroom is also a real treat. Ricotta cheese, traditionally used to stuff pastas such as ravioli and lasagne, also makes an excellent stuffing.

Vegetable Lasagne Primavera with Pasta Substitute

This recipe takes very little time and is excellent for a big family dinner. It's also great for vegetarians.

1. Put two of the eggs, salt, pepper, milk and maize flour in the blender and whizz to a smooth batter.

2. Using a well-greased griddle, pour the batter, fry until firm, and cut into strips 10in long and 2in wide. Turn using an extra large, long spatula. As the strips are cooked, place them in a greased baking dish. When the bottom of the dish is covered, fry the rest of the batter in the same way and save it for topping.

3. In a bowl, mix the ricotta, the remaining eggs, Parmesan, vegetables and parsley. Spread in tablespoonfuls over the strips in the dish. Cover with more of the pasta strips.

4. Pour the white sauce over the dish and cover with shredded mozzarella. Bake for about 12 minutes. Serve hot.

A Versatile Pasta

Any sauce that you would use on wheat pasta can be used on rice pasta – from a rich, creamy Alfredo sauce to a robust marinara sauce.

Serves 6–8

---

4 eggs
½ teaspoon salt (or to taste)
¼ teaspoon pepper (or to taste)
1½ cups milk or water
1 cup maize flour (masa harina)
Butter or oil for greasing the griddle
2 cups chopped raw mixed fresh vegetables, such as spring onions, courgettes, fresh spinach and young peas
½ cup finely chopped fresh parsley
1½ cups Basic White sauce (see page 200)
1lb ricotta cheese
½ cup grated Parmesan cheese
1 cup shredded mozzarella cheese

Chicken in Cider and Apple Brandy

You can prepare this dish in advance.
Reheat when you're ready to serve, adding the cream at the last minute.

Serves 4–6

2 small chickens, cut into
  quarters
4 tablespoons butter
1 cup chopped onion
1 tablespoon cornflour
¼ cup apple brandy or
  Calvados
1¼ cups cider
Salt and pepper to taste
½ cup double cream
Chopped fresh herbs, to serve

1. Rinse and pat the chicken dry. Brown it in butter over a medium heat. Add the onion and cook until softened. Stir in the cornflour.

2. Add the brandy and flame it by setting it on fire with a long match. Be careful not to burn yourself. Add the cider and salt and pepper. Cover and simmer for 25 minutes.

3. Just before serving, place the chicken on a platter. Add the cream to the sauce in the pan, and heat. Spoon the sauce over the chicken, sprinkle with your favourite herbs, and serve.

Shirred Eggs and Asparagus au Gratin

This is a very easy brunch or supper dish.
The trick is arranging the asparagus evenly in the pan.

Serves 4

1lb fresh asparagus,
  trimmed
8 eggs
1 cup crumbled Roquefort
  cheese

1. Blanch the asparagus in boiling water for 5 minutes. Refresh in iced water and drain. Preheat the oven to 180°C/350°F/Gas 4.

2. Butter a gratin dish and arrange the asparagus in the bottom. Break the eggs over the top. Sprinkle with Roquefort and bake until the eggs are done and the cheese is hot and runny (about 12 minutes). Serve hot.

Chapter 5
Poultry

Crispy Potato-Crusted Chicken

Serves 4

12oz potato crisps
4 boneless, skinless chicken
    breasts
⅔ cup sour cream
1 teaspoon freshly ground
    black pepper
2 tablespoons snipped fresh
    chives
1 teaspoon dried thyme

*When you use this crust on your baked chicken, you'll find it's really crispy
and crunchy. Don't add salt as the crisps are already salty.*

1. In a food processor, chop up the potato crisps until you have 1 cup of crumbs.

2. Rinse the chicken breasts, dry on paper towels, and lay them in a greased baking dish.

3. Preheat the oven to 180°C/350°F/Gas 4. Spread the chicken with sour cream, sprinkle with the crisp crumbs mixed with the pepper, chives and thyme, and bake for 25 minutes or until brown and crunchy.

Sporting Chicken Fillets

Serves 4–6

1lb skinless, boneless chicken,
    cut into bite-sized pieces
1 cup potato flour
1 teaspoon salt
Dried red chilli flakes to taste
1 teaspoon baking powder
1 cup fine gluten-free
    cornbread crumbs
1 egg
2 tablespoons milk
Cooking oil as needed

*Tender nuggets of chicken breast in a crisp cornbread crumb coating
make a great snack when you have a crowd.*

1. Rinse the chicken and dry on paper towels, then lay out two sheets of greaseproof paper. Mix together the flour, salt, pepper, and baking powder and spread it on one sheet.

2. Spread the crumbs on the other piece of greaseproof paper. Beat the egg and milk together. Dredge the chicken pieces in the flour mixture, then dip them into the egg mixture, and finally coat them in the crumbs.

3. In a heavy-bottomed frying pan, heat ½in of oil to 185°C/365°F and fry the chicken pieces until golden, about 3–4 minutes. Drain on paper towels.

Classic Southern Fried Chicken

A great fried chicken is perfectly delicious. It's wonderful picnic fare and fabulous when you are giving a sports-on-TV party.

Serves 4

1 chicken, cut into 8 pieces (drumsticks, thighs, breasts and wings)
1 cup buttermilk
1½ cups maize flour (masa harina)
1 teaspoon salt (or to taste)
1 teaspoon black pepper (or to taste)
1 teaspoon baking powder
1 egg, beaten
½ cup gluten-free buckwheat beer
1½ cups cornmeal
Vegetable oil for frying

1. Rinse the chicken pieces and dry on paper towels, then place in a resealable plastic bag with the buttermilk and marinate for 2–3 hours.

2. In a large paper bag, mix together the maize flour, salt, pepper, and baking powder. Add the chicken pieces to the flour mixture one at a time, then close the bag and shake until the chicken is well coated.

3. Whisk the egg and beer together. Spread the cornmeal on a large piece of greaseproof paper. Dip the chicken in the beaten egg/beer mixture. Then roll in the cornmeal, pressing it all together.

4. Bring 1in of oil to 185°C/365°F in a fryer, or heat ½in of oil in a frying pan. Fry the chicken for 20–25 minutes; turn every 4 or 5 minutes. Watch the chicken carefully to make sure that it doesn't burn.

Frying with Maize Flour

When you use maize flour or cornmeal for frying, you can mix it with either rice flour or potato flour for good results. For a light, tempura-like crust, try cornflour mixed with water and egg as a coating. Gluten-free cooking does require a whole new chemistry.

Old-Fashioned Chicken Cacciatore

You can vary this dish by adding fresh mint, red vermouth rather than red wine, capers and lemon zest.

Serves 4–6

1 3½lb chicken, cut into 8
   pieces
1 cup potato or maize flour
   (masa harina)
Salt and pepper to taste
1 teaspoon oregano,
   crumbled
¼ cup olive oil
1 teaspoon butter
1 onion, peeled and diced
2 to 3 cloves garlic, peeled
   and chopped
2 tablespoons fresh rosemary
2 cups mushrooms, chopped
1 16oz jar gluten-free tomato
   sauce or 14oz can
   tomatoes
4oz dry red table wine or to
   taste
½ cup grated Parmesan
   cheese
1 bunch fresh parsley,
   chopped, for garnish

1. Dredge the chicken in the flour, seasoned with salt, pepper and oregano. Heat the oil and butter together until the butter melts. Sauté the chicken in the oil-and-butter mixture. Add the onion, garlic, rosemary and mushrooms. Sauté for 5 minutes.

2. Add the tomato sauce or tomatoes and red wine. Cover and simmer over a very low heat for 1 hour. Remove the chicken to a platter, and continue to simmer the sauce, uncovered, until reduced by half.

3. Spoon the sauce over the chicken and sprinkle with cheese and fresh parsley. Serve with spaghetti squash.

Smooth Chicken and Chicken Liver Paté

This makes great sandwiches on gluten-free toast with pickles on the side.
Or you can serve it with poached eggs for brunch.

1. Heat the butter and oil in a large frying pan. Dredge the livers and chicken in seasoned flour. Sauté for 10 minutes, turning constantly. Place in a food processor. Blend to a purée.

2. Add the garlic and onion to the pan and cook for just a few minutes. Scrape the garlic and onion into the food processor.

3. Deglaze the pan with the brandy, being sure to get up all the browned bits sticking to the bottom of the pan. Pour into the processor. Break eggs and drop into the processor.

4. Pour in the cream at the last minute, and as soon as mixed, turn off the processor.

5. Preheat the oven to 160°C/325°F/Gas 3. Grease a baking tin and pour the mixture into it. Dot the top of the paté with capers and bacon.

6. Place the tin in a larger tin half filled with hot water. Bake for 40 minutes. Cool and slice.

Serves 6–8

2 tablespoons unsalted butter
1 tablespoon olive oil
½lb chicken livers, rinsed and dried
½lb boneless, skinless chicken breasts, cut into small pieces
2 tablespoons tapioca flour or cornflour
Salt and freshly ground white or pink pepper to taste
1 clove garlic, peeled and chopped
¼ cup finely chopped sweet onion
¼ cup brandy
3 large eggs
½ cup double cream
2 tablespoons tiny capers
2 rashers streaky bacon, diced

Indian-Style Chicken with Lentils

Serves 4–6

1 cup lentils
3 cups water
Salt and dried red chilli flakes
  to taste
2 cloves garlic, peeled and
  chopped
1 onion, finely chopped
2 tablespoons lemon juice
1 teaspoon cumin
½ cup chopped fresh parsley
1lb boneless, skinless chicken
  breasts, cut into bite-sized
  pieces
1 cup yogurt
1 tablespoon curry powder
Tabasco sauce to taste

In countries with huge populations, it's both wise and popular to stretch meat, fish and seafood with all kinds of legumes.

1. Place the lentils and water in a saucepan. Bring to the boil, reduce the heat, and simmer.

2. Just before the lentils are cooked (when barely tender, after about 25 minutes), add the salt, chilli flakes, garlic, onion, lemon juice, cumin and parsley.

3. Toss the chicken with the yogurt, curry powder, salt and Tabasco. Place on aluminium foil and grill for 5 minutes on each side.

4. Mix the chicken into the lentils and serve with rice.

Family-Style Turkey Loaf

Serves 4–6

1lb minced turkey
1 cup cornmeal or gluten-free
  cornbread crumbs
⅔ cup milk
¼ cup chilli sauce
3 eggs
1 teaspoon thyme
½ cup chopped onion
Salt and pepper to taste
¼ teaspoon nutmeg
2 rashers streaky bacon

This can be served with rice or mashed potatoes on the side. It can be adapted in many ways to suit the family's tastes, from mild to spicy. For a more grown-up flavour, add 2 tablespoons of brandy.

1. Preheat the oven to 180°C/350°F/Gas 4.

2. Put all the ingredients except the bacon into a food processor and whizz until well blended.

3. Pour into a 9 x 5in loaf tin and put that into a much larger tin. Place in the oven and add boiling water to the larger tin. Cut the bacon rashers in half and arrange across the top of the loaf. Bake for 1 hour.

Elegant Duckling and Fruit-Filled Corn Crêpes

This would be a delicious dinner or lunch served with
baby spinach or fresh salad leaves. The sweetness of the duck works
with the fruit – a marriage made in heaven.

Serves 4

½ cup chicken stock
1 tablespoon cornflour
⅔lb boneless, skinless duck
*   breasts*
½ cup maize flour (masa
*   harina)*
3 tablespoons unsalted butter
Salt and 2 teaspoons freshly
*   ground black pepper*
½ cup dried cranberries
*   soaked in ⅔ cup apple*
*   juice or wine*
¼ cup dried cherries soaked
*   in ½ cup orange juice*
¼ cup chopped celery tops
24 pearl onions
½ cup apple brandy (such as
*   Calvados)*
1 tablespoon dried rosemary,
*   crumbled*
8 large Corn Crêpes (see
*   page 30)*
2 tablespoons butter, melted,
*   or olive oil*

1. Mix the chicken stock and the cornflour and set aside.

2. Dredge the duck breasts in maize flour and sauté them in butter over a medium heat. Add the salt and pepper and the chicken stock/cornflour mixture to the pan, stirring to make a sauce.

3. Add the soaked fruit, celery tops, onions, rosemary and apple brandy. Cover and cook for 20 minutes over a low heat.

4. Preheat the oven to 180°C/350°F/Gas 4.

5. Cool and remove the duck from the pan. Cut it into small pieces and shred. Return the duck to the sauce. Divide the sauce between the 8 crêpes. Roll up the crêpes, place them seam side down in a greased baking dish, and drizzle with melted butter or olive oil. Heat them in the oven for 10–15 minutes. Serve on salad leaves or sautéed spinach.

The Best Roast Turkey

For the sweetest, juiciest bird, try to find a turkey that weighs between 9lb and 12lb. Make extra gravy if required by adding some chicken stock to the basting liquid.

Serves 15

1 10lb turkey
¼lb butter, softened
1 teaspoon dried thyme
½ cup fresh flat-leaf parsley, chopped
Salt to taste and 1 teaspoon pepper
Turkey giblets, including wing tips and neck
½ cup dry white wine
2 bay leaves
1 recipe Stuffing for Roast Turkey (see page 67)
4 rashers streaky bacon
2 teaspoons cornflour
¼ cup water

1. Rinse the turkey in cold water and pat dry. Mix the butter, herbs, salt and pepper thoroughly. Tease it under the skin of the breast, working it into the thighs. Be careful not to tear the skin.

2. Place the giblets and wing tips in a saucepan with the wine and water to cover. Add the bay leaves. Cook for 2 hours, or while the turkey is cooking. Add extra water if it starts to dry out.

3. Stuff the turkey and skewer the legs together. Close the neck cavity with a skewer. Preheat the oven to 160°C/325°F/Gas 3.

4. Place the bacon on the bottom of the roasting tin and start the turkey breast side down. After 30 minutes, turn the turkey over and arrange the bacon over the breast and legs. Roast for 3 hours, basting every 20 minutes with the giblet stock, then with the pan juices. Roast until a meat thermometer reads 70°C/155°F in the thickest part. Leave the turkey to rest for 15 minutes before carving.

5. Make gravy by mixing 2 teaspoons cornflour with ¼ cup water and blending with the pan juices.

Roasting Turkeys

Always start the turkey breast side down so the juices run into, rather than out of, the breast. The bacon prevents the breast from sticking to the roasting tin and adds a nice flavour to the juices. If, like most families, yours likes extra stuffing, make 3–4 cups extra and cook it in a casserole while you are roasting the turkey.

Stuffing for Roast Turkey

Make your own gluten-free cornbread for stuffing a day or two before. Cube it and place in the refrigerator in a plastic bag until ready to use.

1. In a large frying pan, sauté the onion and celery in the butter. Add the sausagemeat and break up with a wooden spoon. Cook until the meat is cooked and the vegetables are tender. Place in a very large bowl.

2. Add the rest of the ingredients to the bowl. With your hands inside large plastic bags, use your hands to mix the ingredients well. Stuff your turkey with this mixture.

Makes stuffing for 1 turkey

1 onion, finely chopped
4 sticks celery with tops, finely
    chopped
2oz butter for frying
1lb gluten-free sausagemeat
10 cups cubed gluten-free
    cornbread
8oz unsalted butter, melted
    with ½ cup water
2 teaspoons dried thyme
10 fresh sage leaves,
    chopped, or 2
    tablespoons dried
2 large tart apples, peeled,
    cored, and chopped
Salt and pepper to taste

Stuffing for Roast Chicken or Duck

*Prunes and nuts go wonderfully well with duck and/or chicken.
They give you the taste of autumn in the country.*

1. Sauté the onion, celery and apples in the butter. When soft, place in a bowl. While the vegetables are sautéing, mix the prunes in a small bowl with the sherry and water to soak.

2. Mix all the ingredients together, tossing. Use this to stuff the bird before roasting.

Makes about 6 cups

1 cup chopped onion
2 cups chopped celery with
    tops
2 apples, peeled, cored and
    chopped
4 tablespoons butter
1 cup pitted prunes, halved
¼ cup dry sherry mixed with
    ½ cup water
3 cups cubed gluten-free
    cornbread
1 tablespoon dried rosemary
2 tablespoons grated orange
    or lemon zest
1 cup walnuts or pecans,
    toasted and chopped
Salt and pepper to taste

Tasty Turkey Parmesan

Serves 4

1¼lb boneless, skinless turkey
    breasts, sliced thinly
1 cup gluten-free cornbread
    crumbs
1 cup grated Parmesan
    cheese
Salt and pepper to taste
1 cup maize flour (masa
    harina)
1 beaten egg
1 cup oil for frying
2 cups fresh tomato sauce
½lb whole-milk mozzarella,
    shredded or thinly sliced

*You can doctor your sauce with extra herbs,
some lemon zest and/or red wine.*

1. Flatten the turkey pieces with a steak mallet. Cut into 4 portions. Mix the cornbread crumbs with half the Parmesan cheese. Dip the turkey in the flour, then in the egg, and finally in the crumb mixture.

2. Preheat the oven to 180°C/350°F/Gas 4.

3. Fry the turkey in oil until golden brown; drain on paper towels. Grease a baking dish. Pour a little tomato sauce into the dish. Add the turkey pieces. Sprinkle with the remaining Parmesan cheese. Cover with tomato sauce. Spread the mozzarella over the top.

4. Bake until hot and bubbling, about 20 minutes. Serve hot.

What's in the Stuffing?

The key to buying gluten-free food is reading every label carefully. Store-bought cornbread stuffing may have wheat flour mixed in with the maize flour and cornmeal. Corn muffins, also a favourite when making homemade stuffing, can have a mixture of wheat flour and cornmeal. In the long run, the safest way to provide gluten-free stuffing is to make cornbread yourself.

Mexican Chicken and Rice

This dish is not too spicy, but it is well seasoned.
Cook the rice while the chicken is simmering.

1. Mix the maize flour, salt and pepper on a sheet of greaseproof paper. Dredge the chicken in it.

2. Heat the oil and brown the chicken in a large pan or Dutch oven. Remove the chicken from the pan.

3. Add the garlic, onion, tomatillos (if obtainable), chilli, sweet pepper and mushrooms. Sauté until soft, about 10 minutes.

4. Add the mushrooms, tomatoes, wine, lemon and cinnamon. Mix well.

5. Return the chicken to the pan and add the short-grained rice and stock. Cover and simmer for 45 minutes. Just before serving, add the parsley or coriander. Serve with rice.

Texas Influence

Mexican cooking is well seasoned, with layers of flavours coming from herbs, aromatic vegetables and, yes, some spices. It's the Texas influence and the American passion for burning up the taste buds that has given Mexican cooking a reputation for being overly spiced.

Serves 4–6

½ cup maize flour (masa harina)
Salt and pepper to taste
1 3½lb chicken, cut in serving-sized pieces, rinsed and dried on paper towels
½ cup corn oil
4 cloves garlic, peeled and cut into thick slices
1 large red onion, chopped coarsely
4 tomatillos, peeled and chopped
1 hot chilli such as serrano or poblano, cored, seeded, and chopped
1 sweet red pepper, cored, seeded, and chopped
10 mushrooms, chopped
1½ cups chopped tomatoes (canned are fine)
1 cup dry red wine
1 lemon, thinly sliced, seeded
½ teaspoon cinnamon
1 cup short-grained rice
2 cups chicken stock
½ cup flat-leaf parsley or coriander, chopped
3 cups cooked white rice, to serve

Spicy Olive Chicken

You can make this easy baked chicken dish all in one pan.
The pan juices will add flavour to the sauce.

Serves 4

1 3lb chicken, cut into 8 pieces
Salt and pepper to taste
4 tablespoons unsalted butter
⅔ cup chopped sweet onion
½ cup chicken stock
½ cup dry white wine
24 green olives, pitted
1 teaspoon prepared Dijon
   mustard
Salt, black pepper and hot
   sauce to taste
Fresh parsley, chopped, for
   garnish

1. Sprinkle the chicken pieces with salt and pepper and brown them in the butter. Sauté the onion in the same pan. Add the stock, wine and olives.

2. Using a fork, whisk in the mustard. Cover the pan and simmer until the chicken is done, about 45 minutes. Add salt, pepper and hot sauce.

3. Pour the sauce and olives over mashed potatoes, rice or rice noodles to accompany the chicken. Garnish with chopped parsley.

Capers

Capers are the flavourful green flower buds of a Mediterranean shrub. They can be bought packed in salt or brine or bottled in vingar. Try to find the smallest – they seem to have more flavour than the big ones. Capers are great on their own or incorporated into sauces. They are also good in salads and as a lively garnish on many dishes that would otherwise be dull.

Chapter 6
Meat Dishes

Stuffed Fillet of Beef with Red Wine Sauce

Serves 10–12

4 tablespoons unsalted butter

4 cups exotic mushrooms
such as criminis, morels,
shiitakes or oysters, stems
removed, chopped finely

6 shallots, peeled and
chopped

4 cloves garlic, peeled and
chopped

1 tablespoon Worcestershire
sauce

¾ cup chestnut flour,
seasoned with salt and
pepper to taste

1 cup dry red wine

4 sage leaves, torn in small
pieces

1 6lb beef fillet, trimmed
of fat

1 tablespoon coarse salt

1 teaspoon black pepper

1 cup beef stock

2 tablespoons olive oil

Stuffing a whole beef fillet with mushrooms and garlic will turn it into a luscious feast. Using chestnut flour adds a nutty and delightful flavour.

1. Melt the butter and sauté the mushrooms, shallots and garlic until the vegetables are soft and the mushrooms are wilted. Add the Worcestershire sauce. Add ¼ cup seasoned flour and blend; stir in half the red wine and the sage. Reduce to about 1½ cups.

2. Preheat the oven to 180°C/350°F/Gas 4.

3. Make a tunnel down the middle of the fillet – use a fat knitting needle or the handle of a blunt knife. Stuff the mushroom mixture into the tube. If there are extra mushrooms, save for the sauce.

4. Coat the outside of the fillet with ½ cup chestnut flour seasoned with salt and pepper. Place the remaining red wine and the beef stock in the bottom of a roasting tin with the fillet. Sprinkle with olive oil and roast for 20 minutes per pound.

Pan Juices Make the Perfect Sauce

Use the pan juices for sauce, served on the side. If they get too reduced, add some boiling water or more beef stock.

Marinated Spicy Beef and Baby Spinach

After you have marinated the beef, the dish takes only a few minutes to cook. Garnish with a few slices of lemon or lime.

ഗ൝

1. In a large bowl or glass baking dish, mix together the garlic, 2 tablespoons sugar, salt, chilli flakes, and 2 tablespoons oil. Add the slices of beef, turning to coat. Cover and refrigerate for 2 hours.

2. Mix together the wine, vinegar, 2 teaspoons sugar and fish sauce; set aside. Heat a nonstick pan over very high heat and add 2 tablespoons oil. Quickly sauté the meat until browned on both sides, about 2 minutes per side. Arrange on a bed of spinach.

3. Add the wine mixture and butter to the pan and deglaze, reducing quickly. Pour over the spinach and meat. Serve with soy sauce and chopped spring onions on the side and slices of lemon or lime.

Fish Sauce

Fish sauce, available from Asian stores, is an important ingredient in Southeast Asian, Chinese and Indonesian cuisines.

Serves 4

2 cloves garlic, chopped
2 tablespoons sugar
½ teaspoon salt, or to taste
1 teaspoon red chilli flakes, or to taste
2 tablespoons canola oil
1½lb beef fillet, trimmed and cut into ½in slices
¼ cup dry white wine
¼ cup white wine vinegar
2 teaspoons sugar
2 tablespoons fish sauce
2 tablespoons canola or groundnut oil
4 cups fresh baby spinach, rinsed, spun dry, stems removed
1 tablespoon butter

For garnish:
Soy sauce, chopped spring onions and lemon and lime slices

Gascony-Style Pot Roast

Serves 6

1 4lb beef topside joint
4 cloves garlic, slivered
1 teaspoon salt
1 teaspoon freshly ground
    black pepper
Pinch each of cinnamon and
    nutmeg
1 rasher streaky bacon, cut
    into pieces
4 shallots, peeled and halved
2 red onions, peeled and
    quartered
2 tablespoons cognac
2 cups red wine
1 cup rich beef stock
1 teaspoon thyme
4 whole cloves
¼ cup cornflour mixed with
    ⅓ cup cold water until
    smooth

This is a traditional holiday dish, often made on Christmas Eve to serve on Christmas Day. Serve with mashed potatoes and winter vegetables.

1. Make several cuts in the meat and put a sliver of garlic in each. Rub the roast with salt, pepper, cinnamon and nutmeg.

2. Heat the bacon in a Dutch oven. Remove the bacon before it gets crisp, and brown the beef in the fat. Surround the beef with shallots and onions. Add the cognac, wine, stock, thyme and cloves.

3. Place in a low oven (120°C/250°F/Gas ½) for 5–6 hours. When the meat is done, place it on a warm platter. Add the cornflour-and-water mixture to the pan juices and bring to the boil. Slice the meat. Serve the sauce over the pot roast with the vegetables surrounding the meat.

A Hearty, Delectable Pot Roast

Crockpots are excellent for cooking a pot roast. Trim the meat well but do leave a bit of fat on it. You can also marinate the meat for a pot roast overnight in red wine and herbs. That will give you a deliciously tender piece of meat.

Thick and Hearty Lancashire Lamb Stew

Make a double quantity and freeze half for another busy day.
Cook beans the old-fashioned way or use canned cannellini beans instead.

&

1. Heat the olive oil in a big, heavy-bottomed stew pot. Dredge the meat with flour seasoned with salt and pepper. Brown the meat, including the bacon. Add the garlic, onions, carrots and bay leaves.

2. When the vegetables are soft, add the stock, wine and herbs. Stir in the lemon juice and zest and the Worcestershire sauce.

3. Cover and cook for 3 hours. Pour off the broth and put in the freezer to bring the fat to the top. When the meat is cool enough to handle, remove from the bones.

4. Return the meat and broth to the pot. If it is too thin, mix 2 tablespoons of cornflour with 3 tablespoons water and add. Bring to the boil.

5. Stir in the beans. Cover and simmer for 20 minutes.

Serves 6

¼ cup olive oil
2lb stewing lamb
½ cup potato flour
Salt and pepper to taste
2 rashers streaky bacon,
    chopped
4 cloves garlic
2 large onions
2 carrots, peeled and chopped
2 bay leaves
2 cups chicken stock
1 cup dry white wine
½ bunch parsley
2 tablespoons dried rosemary
Juice and zest of ½ lemon
2 teaspoons Worcestershire
    sauce
1lb cannellini beans, soaked
    overnight and then
    simmered for 5 hours,
    or 3 13oz cans beans,
    drained

Baby Rack of Lamb with Herb Crust

*This recipe with herbs and cornmeal rather than
white breadcrumbs is just delicious.*

2 racks of lamb, 1½–2lb each,
    most of the fat removed
2 teaspoons salt
Freshly ground black pepper
    to taste
1 cup cornmeal
2 tablespoons dried rosemary
    or 4 tablespoons finely
    chopped fresh
3 tablespoons chopped fresh
    parsley
2 tablespoons chopped chives
2 tablespoons chopped garlic
½ cup olive oil
6 sprigs fresh mint and lemon
    wedges to garnish

1. Preheat the grill to 230C/450°F. Rub the lamb with salt and pepper. Place on a grill pan, bones side up. Grill for 5 minutes.

2. Turn and continue to grill for another 5 minutes. While the lamb is cooking, mix the rest of the ingredients together. Press the herb mixture into the meat. Turn on the oven at 230°C/450°F/Gas 8. Bake the lamb for another 10–12 minutes.

3. Cut into chops and serve.

Snipping Chives

Of course, you can use a knife to chop chives; however, a pair of sharp kitchen scissors works faster and better than a knife. The scissors work well with any number of other ingredients too, such as spring onions and bacon. As with any cutting tool, the sharper, the better – and safer. Dull tools are dangerous – a blunt knife can slip off a tomato, for example – and inefficient.

Greek Lamb-Stuffed Aubergines

*You can do most of this in advance, refrigerate it,
and then put it in the oven for 10 minutes. Serve on beds of lettuce or rice.*

೧೨

**Serves 4 for lunch,
8 as appetizers**

*8 medium aubergines, about
   4–5 in in length*
½ cup olive oil
½ cup chopped onion
4 cloves garlic, chopped
½lb lean ground lamb
Salt and pepper to taste
*½ cup fresh tomato, finely
   chopped*
*3 tablespoons chopped fresh
   mint*
¼ teaspoon ground coriander
Juice of ½ lemon

For garnish:
   *Yogurt, extra mint
   leaves, and finely
   chopped tomato*

1. Fry the whole aubergines in olive oil. When cool enough to handle, make a slit from top to bottom but do not cut through.

2. Over moderate heat, fry the onion, garlic, lamb, salt, pepper, tomato and herbs. Moisten with lemon juice.

3. Keep stirring to blend and break up the lamb. Set aside to cool for 15 minutes. Place the aubergines on a baking sheet covered with aluminium foil. Spread them open and fill with lamb stuffing.

4. Preheat the oven to 200°C/400°F/Gas 6.

5. Bake for 10 minutes. Serve with a dollop of yogurt on each aubergine and garnish with mint and chopped tomato.

Lamb Fat

If you don't like the strong flavour of lamb fat, trim it away before cooking the meat. You can always moisten the lamb with bacon fat, olive oil or butter.

Stuffed Pork Chops

Ask the butcher for thick rib chops, and slit a pocket in each.
The pears become part of the sauce and the thickening is optional.

Serves 4

1 tart apple, peeled, cored,
    and chopped
½ cup chopped onion
1 tablespoon dried
    rosemary, crumbled,
    or 2 tablespoons fresh,
    chopped
¼ cup finely chopped flat-leaf
    parsley
¾ cup olive oil
½ cup gluten-free cornbread
    crumbs
Salt and pepper to taste
4 thick-cut pork rib chops
4 garlic cloves, chopped
2 onions, chopped
½ cup chicken stock
½ cup dry white wine
Zest and juice of ½ lemon
2 ripe pears, peeled, cored
    and quartered
2 teaspoons cornflour mixed
    with 2 tablespoons
    cold water

1. Sauté the apple, onion and herbs in ½ cup olive oil. When softened, add the cornbread crumbs, salt and pepper. When cool enough to handle, stuff into the chops and secure with cocktail sticks.

2. Add the remaining olive oil to the pan and brown the chops over a medium-high heat. Add the rest of the ingredients, except for the cornflour-and-water mixture, and cover. Simmer for 40 minutes over a very low heat.

3. Place the chops on a warm platter and add the cornflour-and-water mixture to the gravy in the pan if you want it to be thicker. Add salt and pepper to taste.

Tenderloin of Pork with Spinach and Water Chestnuts

*For convenience, use fresh baby spinach prewashed and packed in a bag.
Serve this dish with rice.*

Serves 4

*2 pork tenderloins, about
   ¾lb each
¼ cup potato flour
¼ teaspoon nutmeg
¼ teaspoon ground cloves
Salt and pepper to taste
¼ cup olive oil
2 tablespoons lemon juice
1 teaspoon Worcestershire
   sauce
8oz bag fresh baby spinach
½ cup sliced water chestnuts*

1. Trim the pork and cut into portions. On a sheet of greaseproof paper, mix together the flour and seasonings. Dredge the pork with the mixture.

2. Sauté the pork in the olive oil for about 6 minutes on each side; it should be medium.

3. Add the lemon juice, Worcestershire sauce, spinach and water chestnuts. Stir to wilt the spinach. Sprinkle with more olive oil, if the pan is dry.

Buying Pork

You can get 'heirloom' or 'heritage' pork on the Web but pork tenderloin (fillet) is available in almost any supermarket. The tenderloin is about the best and most juicy cut available.

Fruit and Corn-Crusted Pork Tenderloin

Serves 4–6

6 dried apricots, chopped
½ cup dried cranberries
¼ cup sultanas
1 cup warm water
Juice of ½ lemon
2 pork tenderloins, about
    ¾lb each
Worcestershire sauce
1 cup cornmeal
1 teaspoon salt
Freshly ground black pepper
    to taste
½ cup olive oil

The colourful filling makes this a very pretty dish. It is also very flavourful.

1. Put the dried fruit in a bowl with the warm water and lemon juice. Leave to stand until most of the water is absorbed.

2. Preheat the oven to 180°C/350°F/Gas 4.

3. Make a tunnel through each tenderloin using a fat knitting needle or the handle of a blunt knife. Stuff the fruit into the tunnels.

4. Sprinkle the meat with Worcestershire sauce. Make a paste with the cornmeal, salt, pepper and olive oil. Spread it on the pork. Roast for 30 minutes. The crust should be golden brown and the pork pink.

Herb-Stuffed Veal Chops

Serves 4

½ cup chopped shallots
2 tablespoons chopped fresh
    rosemary
2 teaspoons dried basil or
    1 tablespoon chopped
    fresh basil
½ teaspoon ground coriander
2 tablespoons unsalted butter
Salt and pepper to taste
4 thick-cut veal neck chops,
    a pocket cut from the
    outside edge towards the
    bone in each
¼ cup olive oil

This recipe calls for thick-cut chops in which a pocket can be cut for the aromatic herbs and vegetables. The chops can be grilled or sautéed.

1. Sauté the shallots and herbs in butter. Add salt and pepper.

2. Stuff the chops with herbs. Rub chops with olive oil, salt and pepper.

3. Using a barbecue or grill, sear the chops over a high heat. Then, cut the heat to medium for 4–5 minutes on each side for medium chops, depending on the thickness.

Sausage-Filled Veal Roulades

This recipe is easy to double up to serve 8 people.

ᘯᘰ

1. Trim the pounded veal to rough rectangles. In a bowl, mix the sausage-meat, cheese, egg and pepper or, if not of a fine consistency, pulse it in the food processor until it resembles coarse crumbs.

2. Spread the sausage stuffing on the veal and roll up tightly from the wide to the shorter end. Secure with kitchen string.

3. Melt the butter in a pan large enough to hold all the roulades. Turn the veal until lightly browned. Add the stock and cover. Simmer for 30 minutes.

4. Arrange the roulades on a plate. Deglaze the pan with cream and pour the sauce over the veal. Add extra cheese, parsley or watercress to garnish.

Serves 4

8 veal escalopes, pounded
   very thin with a mallet
6oz sausagemeat, crumbled
½ cup grated Parmesan
   cheese
1 egg, beaten
½ teaspoon pepper
2 tablespoons unsalted butter
¼ cup chicken stock
1 cup single cream

Roast Leg of Veal with Mustard Crust

Serves 10–12

½lb unsalted butter, at room
   temperature
½ cup Dijon mustard
1 cup rice or potato flour
1 teaspoon garlic powder
2 teaspoons dried oregano
7lb leg of veal, well trimmed
Salt and pepper
1 cup dry vermouth
Lemon slices

This is a very special occasion entrée. You will probably have to order the veal specially from your butcher – try to get a joint that does not exceed 7lb.

1. Preheat the oven to 200°C/400°F/Gas 6.

2. Make a paste with the butter, mustard, flour, garlic powder and oregano. Rub the veal with salt and pepper. Cover it with the paste.

3. Place the veal in the oven, and add the vermouth. Roast for 15 minutes or until the crust hardens, then reduce the oven temperature to 180°C/350°F/Gas 4.

4. Arrange the lemon slices on top of the veal. Baste every 15 minutes. Roast for 15 minutes per pound. Carve and serve with the pan juices. (Double cream can be added to the pan juices, if you wish, to make a sauce for the meat.)

French Cheese-Filled Veal Roulades

Be creative – you can use any number of stuffings. The stuffing of Boursin cheese and oregano is very spicy, a nice counterpoint to the creamy sauce.

1. Trim the pounded veal to rough rectangles. Combine the Boursin cheese, oregano and egg to make the stuffing. Spread on the veal. Roll up and tie with kitchen string.

2. Melt the butter and lightly brown the veal; add wine and cover. Cook for 30 minutes.

3. Put the roulades on a platter and add cream, Parmesan cheese and nutmeg to the sauce in the pan; heat. Dress and serve.

Pounding Veal

Whether you are cooking escalopes or chops, place the meat between sheets of greaseproof paper and, working from the centre to the edges, pound away! The meat will be very tender after this process.

Serves 4

8 veal escalopes, pounded
   very thin with a mallet
6oz Boursin cheese with black
   pepper
1 teaspoon dried oregano or
   2 teaspoons fresh
1 beaten egg
2 tablespoons butter
½ cup dry white wine
1 cup single cream
¼ cup finely grated Parmesan
   cheese
¼ teaspoon ground nutmeg
   or paprika

Turkish Veal Roulades

*Stuffing the veal with a nice tapenade of olives
and parsley is another excellent choice.*

Serves 4

8 veal escalopes, pounded
   very thin with a mallet
10 pimiento-stuffed green
   olives, chopped
8 black olives (Spanish
   or Greek), pitted and
   chopped
6 spring onions, chopped
½ cup chopped parsley
2 tablespoons olive oil
Juice of ½ lemon
1 egg, beaten
4 tablespoons butter
½ cup dry white wine

1. Trim the pounded veal to rough rectangles. Lay the veal out flat. Mix the olives, spring onions, parsley, olive oil and lemon juice with the beaten egg.

2. Spread the mixture on the veal escalopes. Roll them up and tie with string. Brown in butter. Add wine, cover, and braise over a low heat for 30 minutes. Deglaze the pan with white wine to make the sauce.

Spicy Mixed Meatballs

American meatballs always have bread as a filler and outside coating. Here, we use ground potato crisps. The eggs will hold the balls together, and the ground crisps taste wonderful.

1. In a large bowl, mix all ingredients except 1 cup of the crisp crumbs and the cooking oil.

2. Lay out a large sheet of greaseproof paper. Sprinkle the remaining cup of crisp crumbs on it.

3. Form meatballs, roll them in crumbs, and fry them in oil until well browned. Drain on paper towels and then either refrigerate, freeze, or serve with the sauce of your choice.

Spicy Meatballs

You can add flavour to your meatballs by mincing some dry-cured sausage and mixing it with the beef. Choose a sausage that has aromatics like garlic, and herbs and spices such as anise seeds.

Makes 10–12 meatballs

*1lb mixed minced meat
 – beef, pork, and veal*
2 eggs
2 cloves garlic, chopped
1 teaspoon dried oregano
½ teaspoon cinnamon
½ teaspoon fennel seeds
*½ cup finely grated Parmesan
 cheese*
Salt and pepper to taste
*2 cups crushed low-salt
 potato crisps*
*Light oil, such as canola, for
 frying*

The Best Meat Loaf

This is classic comfort food. With some mashed potatoes and gravy,
your family will love it.

Serves 6–8

1½lb ground beef
½ cup chilli sauce
½ cup milk
3 eggs
1 cup gluten-free cornbread
    crumbs
Salt and pepper to taste
2 garlic cloves, chopped
1 small onion, chopped
1 teaspoon dried rosemary,
    crumbled
2 teaspoons Worcestershire
    sauce
½ teaspoon nutmeg

1. Preheat the oven to 180°C/350°F/Gas 4.

2. Whizz all the ingredients together in a food processor.

3. Grease a 9 x 5in loaf tin. Pour in the meat loaf mixture.

4. Place a roasting tin in the middle of the oven. Put the loaf tin in the larger tin and pour water around it to. Bake for 1 hour and 20 minutes. For an extra touch, drape 2 rashers of streaky bacon over the top of the meat loaf.

A Hot Water Bath

Baking your meat loaf in a hot water bath enables it to stay juicy. The water bath is called a bain-marie, and it keeps baked foods soft, creamy and moist.

Sole Française

Serves 4

4 5oz fillets of Dover sole
    or witch
1 egg
Juice of ½ lemon plus 2
    teaspoons lemon
    juice for the sauce
1 cup rice flour
1 teaspoon salt
1 teaspoon white pepper or
    to taste
½ cup olive oil
2 tablespoons unsalted butter
2oz dry white wine
2 tablespoons capers
½ cup chopped parsley, for
    garnish

*Although classic recipes for this fine dish call for all-purpose flour,
it is much lighter when you use rice flour. You can substitute flounder for sole.*

1. Rinse the sole and set on paper towels to dry.

2. Whisk the egg and juice of ½ lemon together.

3. Mix the flour, salt and pepper on a piece of greaseproof paper. Heat the olive oil in a nonstick pan over a medium-high heat. Dip the pieces of sole in the egg mixture, then in the flour.

4. Sauté the sole until lightly browned, about 3 minutes on each side. Don't overcook or it will fall apart. Place on a warm platter.

5. Mix the butter, wine, and capers in the pan used for the fish. Stirring constantly, bring to the boil, then pour over the fish. Sprinkle with parsley and serve.

Buying Fresh Fish

No matter what the sauce, if a fish is not absolutely fresh, it will taste awful. When you buy fish, it should gleam – the eyes should be very bright and shiny, not glazed, and the scales should be silvery and glistening. But the acid test is to smell it. If it smells anything but fresh, don't buy it. It also helps to make friends with the fishmonger. Ask him questions like, 'When did this come in?' 'What came in this morning?' and 'May I smell that?'

Sole Florentine

*Sole is an adaptable fish; mild and sweet, it goes with many different flavours.
Frozen spinach works fine for this.*

1. Melt the butter over medium heat, and sauté the shallot until softened, about 5 minutes. Blend in the cornflour, cooking until smooth.

2. Add the spinach, cream and nutmeg. Cook and stir until thickened. Pour into a greased baking dish and set aside.

3. Dip the pieces of sole in beaten egg. Then, on a sheet of greaseproof paper, mix the flour, salt and pepper. Dredge the pieces of sole in the flour mixture.

4. Sauté the sole in the olive oil until lightly browned. Arrange over the spinach. Sprinkle with cheese. Run under the grill until very brown and hot, about 3 minutes.

Serves 4

3 tablespoons unsalted butter
1 shallot, chopped
3 tablespoons cornflour
2 10oz packs frozen chopped
    spinach, thawed,
    moisture squeezed out
⅔ cup double cream
¼ teaspoon nutmeg
4 Dover sole fillets, rinsed and
    dried on paper towels
1 egg, well beaten
½ cup rice or potato flour
Salt and pepper to taste
⅔ cup olive oil
¼ cup grated Parmesan
    cheese

Maryland-Style Crab Cakes

Makes 8 crab cakes

½ cup mayonnaise
2 eggs
1 teaspoon Dijon mustard
1 teaspoon Worcestershire
    sauce
Salt and 1 teaspoon red chilli
    flakes, or to taste
1 tablespoon fresh lemon
    juice
1 cup gluten-free cornbread
    crumbs
1¼lb crabmeat
Oil for frying
Lemon wedges to garnish

*If you wish, you can add some diced cooked ham to balance the
sweetness of the crabmeat and give the cakes a great lift.*

1. In a large bowl, mix the mayonnaise, eggs, mustard, Worcestershire
    sauce, salt, chilli flakes and lemon juice. Stir until well mixed.

2. Add half the cornbread crumbs and gently toss in the crabmeat. Form
    8 cakes and coat with more cornbread crumbs.

3. Over a medium heat, bring the oil to 150°C/300°F. Fry the cakes, turn-
    ing after 5 minutes, until golden brown. Serve with lemon wedges.

Topping Off Crab Cakes

*Some cooks add finely chopped onion to their crab cake mixture. Others use
chives. You can also add finely chopped parsley. Some like their crab cakes with
tartare sauce, others with seafood cocktail sauce.*

Marseilles Whipped Cod and Potatoes

*This is a dish that a tired French maman will make at the end of the week.
You can use either salt cod or fresh cod.*

1. If using salt cod, soak the fish overnight in cold water to cover. Change the water once or twice.

2. Boil the potatoes in their skins until a knife slides into the flesh easily. The timing varies according to the size of the potato.

3. Using a long-handled fork, spear the boiled potatoes and peel them. Put the potatoes through a ricer and into a bowl. Whisk in the olive oil and the milk or cream, then add salt and pepper and keep warm.

4. Steam the cod, salted or fresh, for about 15 minutes, until very tender. Make sure there are no bones.

5. Whizz the cod in a food processor until smooth.

6. Fold the cod into the riced potatoes and add the parsley and chives. Blend with a fork until fluffy. Serve hot.

Serves 4

2 cups salt cod, or 1¼lb fresh cod
3 large or 4 medium potatoes, about 2lb
2 tablespoons olive oil
½ cup creamy milk or single cream, use more or less depending on the consistency of the potatoes
Salt and pepper to taste
½ cup each chopped chives and parsley

Cod Grilled on a Bed of Paper-Thin Potatoes

Cod is one of the world's most beloved and versatile fish. It can be baked, grilled, steamed, poached, salted or cooked with milk in a stew.

Serves 4

2lb of waxy potatoes, peeled and sliced paper thin
¼ cup olive oil
2 tablespoons butter, melted
Salt and pepper to taste
4 cod fillets or steaks, about 5oz each
Salt, pepper and butter for the fish
Chopped parsley and lemon wedges to garnish

1. Preheat the oven to 200°C/400°F/Gas 6.

2. In a baking dish, toss the thinly sliced potatoes with oil and melted butter, salt and pepper.

3. Bake the potatoes for 40 minutes or until the top is brown and crisp and the inside soft.

4. When the potatoes are done, lay the fish on top, sprinkle with salt and pepper, dot with butter, and heat the grill.

5. Grill until the fish is done – 8–10 minutes, depending on the thickness of the fish. If the potatoes start to burn, move the dish to a lower shelf in the oven.

6. Sprinkle with chopped parsley and serve with lemon wedges.

Baccalà (Salt Cod) in Thick and Creamy Egg Sauce

This is a very old-fashioned Easter-morning dish. Served over rice or cornbread with hard-boiled eggs in the sauce, it's very satisfying.

∾

Serves 4–6

1lb salt cod, skinless, soaked in cold water for 24 hours, water changed 3 times
2 tablespoons olive oil
¼ cup chopped sweet onion
2 tablespoons butter
2 tablespoons cornflour
½ teaspoon dry mustard
1½ cups milk
¼ cup finely chopped parsley
¼ teaspoon nutmeg
Pepper to taste
2 hard-boiled eggs, chopped
2 pickled cucumbers, finely chopped
8–10 thin slices cornbread, or 4 cups cooked rice

1. Drain the baccalà and cut it into bite-sized pieces. Quickly sauté it in a pan with the olive oil; set aside.

2. Sauté the onion in butter over a medium heat for 6–8 minutes. Blend in the cornflour and dry mustard. Cook for another few minutes and slowly, whisking constantly, blend in the milk. Add the parsley, nutmeg, pepper and chopped egg.

3. Heat, stirring, until very thick. Stir in the cod and keep stirring until very hot. Sprinkle with pickles and serve on cornbread or rice.

Salt Cod

Having come from dire necessity – salted fish would keep during the winter when fishing for fresh fish was impossible – salt cod was looked down on for a time. Now it's viewed with nostalgia, as traditional as any family's food history. Most European countries' cuisines have recipes for salt cod.

Crispy Beer-Battered Fried Prawns

Serves 4

½ cup maize flour (masa
   harina)
¼ teaspoon salt
1 tablespoon butter, melted
1 whole egg
½ cup flat buckwheat beer
1 egg white, stiffly beaten
1¼lb raw prawns, peeled
   and deveined
¼ cup golden rum
2 tablespoons soy sauce
Light oil such as canola, for
   frying

*You can do everything in advance but fry the prawns. Beer batter is delicious
and can be used with other seafood as well as with chicken.*

1. Make the batter in advance by mixing together the first five ingredients. Leave to stand for an hour.

2. Marinate the cleaned prawns in rum and soy sauce for 20 minutes, covered, in the refrigerator.

3. Bring the oil for frying to 190°C/375°F. Add the final egg white to the batter. Dip the prawns in the batter a few times to coat. Gently lower a few prawns at a time into the oil. Fry for about 4 minutes, or until well browned. Drain on paper towels and serve.

Golden Sautéed Scallops

This recipe calls for caramelizing the scallops. Now, that's absolutely terrific.
And it tastes wonderful. You'll find lots of excuses to serve these.

ରେ

1. On a sheet of greaseproof paper, mix the flour, sugar, salt and pepper. Roll the scallops in the flour mixture.

2. Heat the butter and oil over a medium-high heat. Add the scallops and watch them. They will brown quickly. Cook for 2–3 minutes on each side. Serve with any of your favourite sauces.

Serves 4

½ cup maize flour (masa harina)
2 tablespoons white sugar
1 teaspoon salt
½ teaspoon white pepper
1½lb large scallops, each about 2 in across
2 tablespoons unsalted butter
2 tablespoons olive oil

Savoury Shark and Bacon

Shark is a melt-in-your-mouth kind of fish –
and it really deserves to be cooked more often. It is sweet and tender.

ରେ

1. Preheat the grill to 230°C/450°F. Mix the chilli sauce, orange juice, Worcestershire sauce, lemon juice, and Tabasco sauce in a small bowl.

2. Rinse and pat the shark steaks dry. Sprinkle with salt and pepper. Paint them with the sauce mixture.

3. Place them on an oiled grill pan. Arrange the bacon on top of the shark and grill for 3 minutes. Turn the bacon and grill for 2 more minutes. Turn off the grill and close the oven door to let the shark cook through, about 6 minutes.

Serves 4

2 tablespoons chilli sauce
1 tablespoon concentrated orange juice
1 tablespoon Worcestershire sauce
Juice of ½ lemon
1 teaspoon Tabasco sauce, or to taste
1¼lb boneless shark steak, cut into portions
Salt and pepper to taste
4 rashers streaky bacon

Chinese Prawn Balls

Serve with hot mustard or any other Asian sauce.
For a variation, serve with tartare sauce.

1lb raw prawns, peeled and
    deveined
1 egg
1 tablespoon dry sherry
2 teaspoons soy sauce
1 teaspoon sugar
1 tablespoon cornflour
1 cup lean ground pork
2 spring onions, chopped
3 cups oil for frying

1. Adding slowly, place the ingredients, except the cooking oil, in the food processor. Pulse, and scrape the sides often.

2. Heat the oil to 170°C/360°F. Carefully drop balls of the mixture by the teaspoonful into the oil. When golden, after about 3 to 4 minutes, place them on a serving platter lined with paper towels or napkins to drain. Serve and enjoy.

Using Fresh Prawns

Never use precooked prawns for cooking. They will be rubbery and tough. Cooked prawns are pink; raw prawns are greyish or white. It may be a bit of trouble to peel and clean them, but it's well worth it to get the succulent flavour of good fresh prawns.

Southern Fried Oysters

These are so crunchy on the outside and succulent on the inside,
you will probably have to make an extra batch.
Serve with any of the sauces in this chapter or just a squeeze of lemon juice.

1. Place the oysters in a colander to drain. Thoroughly mix the flour, corn-meal, baking powder, nutmeg, salt and pepper.

2. Dip the oysters in the egg and then in the flour-and-cornmeal mixture. Bring the oil in the pot to 190°C/375°F and fry for about 3–4 minutes or until browned.

3. Remove with a slotted spoon. Drain on paper towels.

Seafood Loves to Be Saucy

Even the tastiest of molluscs and crustaceans love to be dipped or bathed in sauces. And there are a variety of options and substitutions. Any citrus can be substituted for just about any other, for example, limes for lemons, grapefruit for orange, and you can blend them together for intriguing outcomes using your own original flair for flavours. Throw in some ginger, curry powder, or mustard and you'll add another layer of flavour.

Serves 4

24 oysters, shucked
½ cup maize flour (masa harina)
1 cup cornmeal
1 teaspoon baking powder
¼ teaspoon nutmeg
½ teaspoon salt or to taste
Freshly ground black pepper to taste
2 beaten eggs
Oil for deep frying

Spicy Dipping Sauce for Prawns and Oysters

Makes 1½ cups

1 cup chilli sauce
1 teaspoon orange bitters
2 teaspoons lemon juice
1 teaspoon grated
    horseradish or to taste
1 teaspoon chopped fresh
    gingerroot
1 teaspoon brown sugar, or
    to taste
1 teaspoon cider vinegar
½ teaspoon garlic powder
Salt and pepper to taste

A good dipping sauce has dozens of uses.
Make in advance and store in the refrigerator.

Place all the ingredients in the blender and whizz until well blended.

Citrus Dipping Sauce for Prawns and Oysters

Makes 1½ cups

½ cup marmalade
¼ cup soy sauce
¾ cup fresh orange juice
1 teaspoon Dijon mustard
Juice of ½ lime
Juice of ½ lemon
1in fresh ginger, peeled and
    chopped
Salt and pepper to taste

One of the best things about this sauce is its versatility.
You can use it with fried scallops, cold seafood or chicken.

Place all the ingredients in a saucepan and boil until well blended. Cool and store in the refrigerator.

Seafood à la King

*You can make the sauce the day before and
add the seafood at the last minute. Serve with rice or stuff into crêpes.*

ᔐᔑ

1. Sauté the shallots in the butter over a moderate heat for 5 minutes. Add the mushrooms and pearl onions. Stir, cooking for a few more minutes.

2. Mix the cornflour with cold water and add to the pan, stirring to blend. Blend in the tomato paste and brandy. Warm the cream slightly, then stir it into the sauce in the pan. (You can prepare this dish in advance up to this point. Store in the refrigerator until ready to serve.)

3. Reheat the sauce but do not boil. Taste for salt and pepper and add the seafood. When the prawns turn pink, the dish is done. Garnish with caviar and serve.

Long Live the King!

This dish was created at the Brighton Beach Hotel on Long Island, New York, by Chef George Greenwald for his boss, E. Clarke King, II. It became very popular when Campbell's brought out their canned cream of mushroom soup, which was used as a base.

Serves 4

½ cup shallots, chopped
¼ cup unsalted butter
20 small white mushrooms, cut in half
20 pearl onions, fresh or frozen, cut in half
2 tablespoons cornflour
2 tablespoons cold water
1 tablespoon tomato paste
2 tablespoons brandy
1½ cups cream
Salt and pepper to taste
½lb raw prawns, cleaned and deveined
½lb scallops
2 tablespoons red salmon caviar for garnish

Lobster and Prawn Salad

Serves 4

1 cup mayonnaise
1 teaspoon Dijon mustard
Juice of ½ lime and
    1 teaspoon zest
1 teaspoon soy sauce
1 tablespoon chilli sauce
1 teaspoon chopped garlic
Salt and pepper to taste
Meat of 1 small (1½lb) lobster,
    cooked
½lb cleaned and cooked
    prawns
¼ cup mixed, snipped
    fresh dill, and chopped
    fresh parsley
1 tablespoon capers
Shredded lettuce

Try using different citrus fruits and mixing in different vegetables. Use almonds instead of peanuts. And if you like coriander, use that instead of parsley.

1. Mix together the mayonnaise, mustard, lime juice and zest, soy sauce, chilli sauce, chopped garlic, salt and pepper.

2. Just before serving, mix the sauce with the seafood. Garnish with snipped fresh dill and chopped parsley, sprinkle with capers, and serve on a bed of lettuce.

Capers

The islands of the Mediterranean are lush with the bushes that produce capers and they are used in profusion in many fish, meat and salad dishes. The French love them, as do the Italians, Greeks, Sardinians and Maltese. Try some capers in a butter sauce poured over a piece of fresh sea bass and you'll understand their popularity.

Poached Monkfish in Caper Butter Sauce

Monkfish is a mild, sweet fish that is wonderful cooked in many ways.
It is delicious poached, grilled or baked.

Serves 4

1½lb monkfish, cut in
4 portions
½ cup potato flour
2 tablespoons olive oil
¼ cup dry white wine
¼ cup chicken stock
1 tablespoon butter
2 tablespoons capers
Salt and pepper to taste
Paprika and lemon wedges
for garnish

1. Dredge the fish in flour, then sauté over medium heat in olive oil. Turn after 4 minutes.

2. Add the wine, stock, butter and capers. Poach for about 8 minutes, or until the fish is cooked through. Place the fish on a warm plate, reduce the sauce by half and pour over the fish.

3. Sprinkle with salt, pepper and paprika. Serve with lemon wedges.

Monkfish – Poor Man's Lobster

Oddly enough, monkfish was once considered a throwaway fish! It has a slightly hooded flange around its head, like a monk's cowl. It loves various sauces. The only thing to remember is not to overcook it. Monkfish, when poached in clam juice, water or white wine, puffs, growing lighter and fluffier. Then all you have to do is add lemon and butter, and it's very much like lobster.

Mussels Marinière

This is a thick, creamy stew.
It's absolutely delicious and perfectly quick and simple to make.

Serves 4

½ cup finely chopped onion
2 tablespoons butter
2 tablespoons cornflour
1 cup dry white wine
½ cup celery tops, chopped
3–4lb mussels, scrubbed and
    debearded
1 cup double cream
Salt and pepper to taste
Juice of ½ a lemon
½ cup fresh flat-leaf parsley,
    chopped

1. Sauté the onion in the butter until soft. Work in the cornflour. Whisk in the white wine and add the celery tops. Mix and bring to the boil.

2. Pour in the prepared mussels. Cover and continue to boil. After 2 minutes, stir to bring the bottom ones up.

3. Have ready a large serving bowl at the side of the pot. Remove the mussels as they open.

4. When all of the mussels are open and removed from the pot, reduce the heat and add the cream. Heat but do not allow to boil. Add salt and pepper to taste.

5. Pour over the mussels; sprinkle with lemon juice and parsley. Serve in warm bowls with a big bowl for the shells.

Check Your Mussels

You must be sure that your mussels are alive. This means they are shut tightly and when you tap two together, you get a sharp click, not a hollow thump. Often, they will be slightly open but close when tapped – that's fine. Just don't use any that are cracked, open, or hollow-sounding. The same is true for clams. Always scrub clams and mussels with a stiff brush under cold running water.

Chapter 8
Vegetarian Entrées

Stuffed Artichokes with Lemon and Olives

Artichokes have a way of making everything around them taste delicious. They can be eaten with just a little butter or mayonnaise or lemon juice.

Serves 4 as an entrée or 8 as an appetizer

4 large artichokes, trimmed and split lengthwise
½ lemon
1 cup cooked rice
10 green olives, chopped
10 kalamata olives, chopped
2 tablespoons chopped parsley
3 tablespoons butter or margarine, melted
1 teaspoon garlic salt
Pepper to taste
1 egg, optional

1. Boil the artichokes in 8 pints of water with lemon and rind, squeezed, for 20 minutes. Drain and lay on a baking sheet, cut side up.

2. Preheat the oven to 180°C/350°F/Gas 4. Mix together the rest of the ingredients (including the egg, if using) in a large bowl.

3. Spoon the filling over the artichokes, pressing between the leaves. Bake for 15 minutes, until hot.

Grilled Portobello Mushrooms

These big, meaty mushrooms are great sliced over salad, stuffed or chopped into sauce.

Serves 4

4 large (4–5in in diameter) portobello mushrooms, stems removed
1 cup balsamic vinaigrette
Salt and pepper to taste

1. Marinate the mushrooms in the vinaigrette for 1-2 hours, covered, in the refrigerator.

2. Preheat the barbecue to glowing coals, or set the grill to low.

3. Grill the mushrooms, then slice and serve.

Mushrooms and Protein

Mushrooms are not really high in protein but they are filling. Large portobello mushrooms are great for grilling or stuffing with all kinds of goodies. They make excellent bases for rice, quinoa, eggs and vegetables.

Stuffed Peppers with Veggie-Burger Filling and Spices

*Veggie burgers are a boon to the vegetarian cook.
They are generally well seasoned and quite delicious.*

Serves 4

4 large garlic cloves, chopped
1 large onion, chopped
¼ cup olive oil
1 tablespoon sesame oil
1lb veggie burgers
Salt and pepper to taste
4 large green or red peppers

1. Sauté the garlic and onion in the olive and sesame oil until soft. Add the veggie burgers, breaking up with a wooden spoon. Add salt and pepper.

2. Preheat oven to 180°C/350°F/Gas 4.

3. Cut the peppers in half lengthwise and scoop out the seeds and cores. Fill with the burger mixture. Place on an oiled baking sheet.

4. Bake for 25 minutes. Serve hot.

Dry Veggie Burgers?

You can do several things to keep veggie burgers moist. Mixing a little chopped fresh tomato into the mix is one option. Another solution is to add olive oil, milk or cream before grilling. A bit of cooked, mashed potato also adds bulk and moisture. Add about a tablespoon of tomato, oil, milk or mashed potato per burger.

Stuffed Aubergine with Ricotta and Spices

This dish is also known as Aubergine Sicilian.
It freezes beautifully and is very delicious.

Serves 4

2 medium aubergines,
    peeled, cut in 16 round
    slices (8 each) and salted
1 cup rice or maize flour
    (masa harina)
Freshly ground black pepper
    to taste
¼ cup olive oil, or as needed
2 cups tomato sauce
1lb ricotta cheese
1 cup grated Parmesan
    cheese
2 eggs
1 tablespoon dried oregano
1 cup shredded mozzarella
    cheese

1. Stack the salted aubergine slices on a plate and put another plate with a weight on top to press the brown liquid out of them.

2. Mix the flour and pepper and use it for dredging the aubergine slices. Fry the slices in the olive oil, removing them to paper towels to drain as they are browned.

3. Preheat the oven to 160°C/325°F/Gas 3. Grease a 4-pint casserole dish or a 10 x 10in glass dish and spread with a thin layer of tomato sauce.

4. In a large bowl, mix the ricotta cheese, half the Parmesan, eggs and oregano. Place a tablespoon of the egg and cheese mixture on each slice of aubergine and roll up, placing seam side down in the baking dish.

5. Spread with sauce, sprinkle with the rest of the Parmesan and the mozzarella, and bake for 35 minutes.

Smaller Is Sweeter

The smaller aubergines now available are much sweeter than the very large ones and not old enough to have grown bitter. Also, many have few seeds. They come in pale cream, lavender, and purple, all the way from egg-sized to long and skinny. All are good!

Stuffed Portobello Mushrooms with Roasted Tomatoes and Quinoa

You can substitute rice for quinoa.
However, you get a nice nutty flavour from the quinoa.

∽

1. Preheat the oven to 180°C/350°F/Gas 4. Place the mushrooms on a well-greased baking dish.

2. Sprinkle the tomatoes with oil and garlic. Roast them in the oven for 20 minutes or until soft.

3. Mix the roasted tomatoes with the cooked quinoa, nuts, butter or margarine and seasonings. Add optional ingredients if desired. Spoon into the mushrooms.

4. Bake the mushrooms for 30 minutes or until very hot and soft.

Do You Know Quinoa?

Rich, nutrient-filled quinoa is considered a 'supergrain' though it is not really a grain but the starchy seed of a plant related to spinach. The protein in quinoa is more complete than that of other grains, and contains the amino acid lysine, as do buckwheat and amaranth. The quality of quinoa's protein is equivalent to that of milk.

Serves 4

4 portobello mushrooms, about 4–5in in diameter, stems removed
16 cherry tomatoes, cut in half
¼ cup olive oil
1 tablespoon chopped garlic
2 cups cooked quinoa
¼ cup walnuts, finely chopped (almonds or pecans are fine)
4 tablespoons butter or margarine, melted
1 teaspoon turmeric
Salt and red chilli flakes to taste
¼ cup capers (optional)
¼ cup sultanas (optional)
1 teaspoon lemon zest (optional)

Stuffed Portobello Mushrooms with Roquefort and Sweet Red Peppers

Serves 4

4 large whole portobello mushrooms, marinated in balsamic vinaigrette
8 tablespoons crumbled Roquefort cheese
4 roasted red peppers, cut in strips (from a jar is fine)
Salt and pepper to taste

This is as good as it gets. Serve with salad or in an omelette.

1. Preheat the oven to 180°C/350°F/Gas 4. Place the marinated mushrooms on a baking sheet.

2. Place 2 tablespoons cheese in each mushroom. Put the pepper strips on top. Sprinkle with salt and pepper. Bake for about 20 minutes, until the cheese melts.

Indian Vegetable Cakes

Serves 4–6

1 tablespoon olive oil
1 10oz pack frozen chopped spinach, thawed and squeezed of excess moisture
5oz frozen petit pois, thawed
½ bunch spring onions, chopped
1 teaspoon curry powder
Salt and hot pepper sauce to taste
¼ cup cornmeal
5 extra large eggs, well beaten
½ cup grated Parmesan cheese

This is a great way to get kids to eat their veggies! A nonstick pan helps to prevent sticking. Sour cream makes a very good garnish.

1. Heat the olive oil in a nonstick pan over a medium flame. Mix together all the ingredients except the Parmesan cheese.

2. Drop patties, 3 or 4 at a time, into the pan and fry, turning, until delicately browned. Sprinkle with cheese.

Sweet Potato Gratin with Leeks and Onions

*The combination of sweet and savoury makes this a
fascinating, unique and delicious dish.*

1. Sauté the leeks, onions, and celery in olive oil or butter. Preheat the oven to 160°C/325°F/Gas 3. Grease an oval metal or ceramic gratin dish.

2. Layer the sweet potato slices in the gratin dish with the vegetables. Sprinkle with thyme, salt and pepper as you go along.

3. Finish with a layer of potatoes. Add the milk until it meets the top layer of potatoes. Then add the cornbread crumbs. Dot with extra butter or margarine.

4. Bake until the potatoes are soft, about 1 hour. Add more milk if it starts to dry out.

Serves 4–6

2 leeks, white part only, chopped
2 large sweet onions such as Vidalias, chopped
2 sticks celery with tops, finely chopped
4 tablespoons olive oil or butter
1 teaspoon dried thyme
4 sweet potatoes, peeled and sliced thinly
Salt and pepper to taste
Milk to cover
1½ cups gluten-free cornbread crumbs
Butter or margarine for topping

Corn and Spinach Pockets
Stuffed with Cheese and Artichokes

Serves 8

1 10oz jar or can artichoke
   hearts
1 10oz pack frozen spinach,
   thawed, moisture
   squeezed out
1 cup ricotta cheese
4oz cream cheese
¼ cup chopped chives
¼ teaspoon freshly ground
   nutmeg
Salt and pepper to taste
1 egg
8 large (8 to 9in in diameter)
   Corn Crêpes (page 30)
Beaten egg for sealing
   pockets

*This is one of the creative and exciting vegetarian and
gluten-free dishes you can make with Corn Crepes (page 30).*

1. Whizz the artichoke hearts in a food processor with the spinach, slowly adding the cheeses, chives, seasonings and egg.

2. Preheat oven to 180°C/350°F/Gas 4. Lay out the crêpes on a nonstick baking sheet or one covered with a sheet of aluminium foil.

3. Divide the filling among the crêpes, spooning on to one half and leaving the other half plain.

4. Wet the rims of the crêpes with beaten egg. Fold over and press lightly to seal, and then bake for 20 minutes or until they are well browned and the filling is bubbling out.

Selecting and Preparing Fresh Artichokes

Look for artichokes that are tightly closed. Take a pair of kitchen scissors and clip off the sharp points. You can use a knife to cut off the tops. They are hearty when stuffed with many kinds of delicious foods. If you eat fish, salmon mixed with rice makes an excellent stuffing.

Spinach with Baked Eggs and Cheese

*This is an excellent brunch, lunch or supper. Everyone loves it,
and even after a tough day, it's easy to put together.*

1. Preheat the oven to 160°C/325°F/Gas 3. Butter a 10 x 10in glass baking dish and sprinkle it with cornbread crumbs.

2. Mix the spinach, butter, cheese, nutmeg, salt and pepper together. Stir in the double cream. Spread the spinach-cheese mixture in the bottom of the prepared dish.

3. Using the back of a tablespoon, make 8 depressions in the spinach mixture. Nestle the raw eggs in the holes. Bake for 20 minutes or until the eggs are firm but not hard.

Serves 4

1½ cups gluten-free cornbread crumbs
3 10oz packs frozen spinach, thawed, moisture squeezed out
2 tablespoons butter or margarine, melted
½ cup shredded Gruyère cheese
½ teaspoon nutmeg
Salt and pepper to taste
1 cup double cream
8 eggs

Crispy Potato Pancakes

4 potatoes, peeled and
   coarsely grated
2 mild onions, chopped fine
2 eggs, well beaten
½ cup potato flour
Salt and pepper to taste
2 cups cooking oil (such as
   canola)
Sour cream, apple sauce,
   fruit preserves, salsa or
   chutney to garnish

*This is basically a good, old kosher recipe. It is marvellous with apple sauce,
sour cream or both. For brunch, it's excellent with eggs on the side.*

1. Mix the grated potatoes, onions and eggs in a bowl. Sprinkle with potato flour, salt and pepper.

2. Heat the oil to 180°C/350°F and spoon in the potato cakes, pressing down to make patties.

3. Fry until golden, about 5 minutes on each side. Drain, keep warm, and serve with the garnish of your choice.

The Origins of Potato Pancakes

During the long winters in northern and eastern Europe, when fresh fruits and vegetables were not available, winter storage of carrots, potatoes, beets, Brussels sprouts, apples and dried fruits was crucial to prevent scurvy, or ascorbic acid deficiency. As Mother Nature would have it, these vegetables are packed with vitamins and minerals. Potato pancakes with sour cream, apple sauce or fruit syrups became a staple in harsh climates.

Potato Frittata with Cheese and Herbs

Use a heavy nonstick pan for this recipe, or the starch in the potatoes will stick. You can experiment with different herbs and cheeses.

Serves 4

1 large waxy potato, peeled
4 teaspoons butter
Salt and pepper to taste
6 eggs
½ cup grated Parmesan
    cheese
6 sage leaves, chopped
Fresh herbs, extra cheese,
    sour cream to garnish

1. Using a mandolin, slice the potato as thinly as possible. Melt the butter in a heavy 12in pan.

2. Add the potato in a thin layer, and season with salt and pepper. Cook over a medium heat for 10 minutes – this will be the crust.

3. Beat the eggs well; add the cheese and chopped sage. Pour over the potato slices and turn down the heat to the lowest possible setting. Cook for 10 minutes. Preheat the grill.

4. When the eggs have set, put the frittata under the grill until golden brown on top. Cut into wedges and serve at once with garnishes.

Frittata with Asparagus and Two Cheeses

*Some matches are made in heaven, and asparagus with eggs
and cheese is a divine combination.*

Serves 4

¾lb fresh asparagus
2 tablespoons butter
6 eggs
1 cup grated Cheddar cheese
¼ cup shredded Monterey
   jack or Gruyère cheese
1 teaspoon lemon rind,
   grated
Salt and pepper to taste

1. Trim off the woody ends of the asparagus and steam for 10 minutes; drain and chop.

2. Melt the butter in a heavy 12in pan over a medium-high heat. Beat the eggs; mix in the cheeses, lemon rind, salt and pepper.

3. Pour the egg and cheese mixture into the pan, distribute the asparagus, and reduce the heat, cooking very slowly for 10–15 minutes. Meanwhile, preheat the grill.

4. Flash under the grill for 10 seconds, or until nicely browned.

Use Up Your Leftovers

The frittata is a staple in Italy – putting a lot of eggs together with leftover or fresh vegetables is a fine way of using every precious bit of food. A frittata can be jazzed up with herbs, cheeses and hot red chilli flakes. Or it can be child-mild for young kids. The only thing to remember about frittatas is that just about anything goes!

Fried Potato Balls

You can hide surprises inside these treats,
such as olives, halved cherry tomatoes or cubes of cheese.

Make 8 to 12 balls

3 eggs separated, whites
*   stiffly whipped*
1¾ cup finely grated
*   Parmesan cheese*
¼ cup potato flour, more if
*   the mixture is soft or wet*
Salt and pepper
1½ cups boiled mashed
*   potatoes*
2 cups oil for frying

1. Beat the egg yolks, 1 cup of the Parmesan cheese, flour, salt and pepper into the potatoes. Fold in the egg whites.

2. Form into balls about the size of large marbles. Roll in Parmesan cheese. If too soft, place on a baking sheet in the freezer for a few minutes.

3. Heat the oil to 190°C/375°F. Carefully add the potato balls and fry until well browned.

4. Be careful not to let the oil get too hot. Drain the potato balls on paper towels, and serve hot.

Tofu and Vegetables with Macadamia Nuts and Asian Citrus Sauce

Serves 4

1 tablespoon sesame seed oil

3 tablespoons groundnut or other vegetable oil

1 bunch spring onions, chopped

1in piece ginger, peeled and chopped

⅔lb sugar snap peas, ends trimmed

2 cups mung bean sprouts

2 cups shredded Chinese cabbage

½ orange, juice and rind, pulsed in the food processor

1 teaspoon Chinese five-spice powder

1 teaspoon Chinese mustard or Japanese wasabi, or to taste

¼ cup sake or dry white wine

¼ cup light soy sauce

1lb tofu, cubed

This is an elegantly flavoured dinner with contrasting textures. Serve with rice.

1. Heat the oils in a wok. Add the spring onions and ginger. Lightly mix in the rest of the vegetables and toss in the oil for 3–4 minutes. Place the vegetables in a large, warm serving bowl.

2. Mix together the orange juice and rind, five-spice powder, mustard, sake and soy sauce.

3. Stir into the wok until blended. Add the tofu cubes and return the vegetables to the wok; mix to coat with the sauce. Serve hot.

A Source of Protein for Vegetarians

Tofu, long used in Asia because meat and milk were both scarce and expensive, has become an important part of the vegetarian diet. It can be flavoured to taste like many kinds of meat. Or it can be sweetened and prepared with fruit for desserts. It's delicious in soups and with vegetables.

Spinach-and-Cheese-Stuffed Baked Potatoes

This is an American favourite, and if you enjoy anchovies,
they make a delightful addition to this recipe.

Serves 4 as a meal,
8 as a snack

4 Idaho or Yukon Gold
*   potatoes*
1 (10-ounce) package frozen
*   chopped spinach, thawed*
*   and moisture squeezed out*
1 cup sour cream
¼ teaspoon nutmeg
1 cup grated processed
*   cheese*
Salt and pepper to taste
½ cup grated mature
*   Cheddar cheese*

1. Preheat the oven to 180°C/350°F/Gas 4.

2. Bake the potatoes for 40 minutes. Then cool the potatoes and split them in half lengthwise.

3. Spoon out the insides of the potatoes and place in a bowl; add the spinach. Stir in the sour cream and nutmeg. Add the processed cheese. Season to taste with salt and pepper.

4. Restuff the potato skins. Arrange the Cheddar cheese on top. Bake for another 20 minutes and serve hot.

Sweet Pepper and Gorgonzola Omelette

Serves 2

2 teaspoons unsalted butter
4 eggs, well beaten
2oz crumbled Gorgonzola
    cheese
4 x 2in strips roasted red
    pepper
Salt and hot red chilli flakes
    to taste

This omelette has a delightful flavour from the Gorgonzola cheese melting into the eggs. A nonstick pan takes all the guesswork out of making omelettes.

1. Heat a 10in nonstick pan over a medium-high heat. Melt the butter and swirl to coat. Add the eggs and swirl to distribute evenly in the pan.

2. Place the cheese and pepper strips on one side of the omelette. Season with salt and chilli flakes.

3. Cook until just set, when it has the consistency of custard (soft and creamy but not liquid or runny). Flip the plain side over the side with the cheese and peppers. Cut in half and serve on a warmed plate.

Eggs

Eggs are a versatile, all-purpose protein source. Omelettes can solve any number of nutritional problems, plus providing something really easy to digest and great for finicky appetites. Various vegetables, cheeses and herbs make perfect fillings for omelettes. The more creative the combination, the more interesting the omelette.

Chapter 9
Rice and Wild Rice

Persian Rice with Saffron and Sour Cherries

Serves 6–8

1 tablespoon butter or
  olive oil
1½ cups basmati or other
  short-grain rice
2½ cups chicken stock
1 teaspoon saffron threads
1 8oz jar sour cherries,
  with juice
1 tablespoon butter
1 teaspoon salt
Freshly ground pepper to
  taste
½ cup slivered almonds,
  toasted, for garnish

This is excellent with duckling, turkey or chicken. It has a slight bite to it and a nice tang. It's a simple recipe but most delicious, supplied by an Iranian friend.

1. Heat the butter or oil and add the rice; cook, stirring, for 6 minutes.

2. Add the chicken stock and bring to the boil. Reduce the heat to low and add all but the nuts.

3. Cover and simmer for 25 minutes, or until the rice is tender. Check the rice every 10 minutes to make sure it does not dry out. If the rice is stubbornly tough, add more stock or water.

4. Place in a warm serving bowl and sprinkle with almonds.

Rice and Fruit

You can also use canned unsweetened sour cherries or fresh sour cherries, but do not use sweet cherries in this recipe. Interestingly, you can use summer fruit, tropical fruit, dried fruit and just about any kind of nut with white rice or wild rice.

Hawaiian-Style Rice with Pineapple, Mango, and Macadamia Nuts

*This is perfect with grilled or roasted ham, pork chops, or pork tenderloin.
You can also add crumbled crisp bacon as an interesting garnish.*

༄

1. Bring the water and juice to the boil. Stir in the rice and return to the boil. Cover and simmer for 30 minutes, or until the rice is tender.

2. Add the rest of the ingredients except the butter and nuts, reheat, and serve hot with butter and nuts arranged over the top.

Serves 4–6

1 cup water
1½ cups orange juice
1½ cups short-grained rice
Grated zest of 1 orange
1 teaspoon salt
Tabasco sauce to taste
½ cup chopped pineapple
1 ripe mango, diced
2 tablespoons butter
½ cup toasted macadamia
nuts, for garnish

Wild Rice with Dried Cranberries and Shallots

*This is exquisite with venison or rabbit.
You can cook the rice in water or beef stock.*

༄

1. Bring the water to the boil and add the rice; return to the boil and lower the heat to a simmer. Add salt and pepper. Cover tightly and simmer until the rice is cooked. Check the rice for moisture and add liquid whenever necessary.

2. In a separate sauté pan, melt the butter and add shallots; cook over a medium heat until soft but not brown. Add the rosemary and remove from the heat.

3. When the rice is tender, add the butter, shallots and rosemary. Stir in the cranberries and port. Taste and adjust seasonings if needed. Add the garnish and serve warm or hot.

Serves 6

4 cups water or beef stock
¾ cup wild rice
1 teaspoon salt or to taste
freshly ground pepper to
taste
2 tablespoons butter
4 shallots, chopped
2 tablespoons fresh rosemary,
stripped from stems, or 1
tablespoon dried
½ cup dried cranberries
soaked in ⅔ cup port
or other red wine for 30
minutes or until softened
Chopped celery tops, parsley,
or other herbs to garnish

Rangoon Rice Cakes

Serves 6

6 cups cooked rice
½ cup chopped red onion
1 clove garlic, chopped
1in fresh ginger, peeled and
  chopped
1 tablespoon Madras curry
  powder
½ teaspoon cinnamon
2 eggs
½ cup double cream
1 teaspoon salt and black
  pepper to taste
¼–½ cup cooking oil, as
  needed
2 cups dry gluten-free
  breadcrumbs
½ cucumber, chopped
½ cup yogurt
juice of ½ lemon
12 mint leaves for garnish

*These are spicy and need a nice cold cucumber salad or
some chutney on the side. Serve with chicken, prawns or fish.*

1. Mix the rice, garlic, onion, ginger and spices together.

2. Add the eggs and cream and keep mixing. Sprinkle with salt and pepper to taste and combine well.

3. Form into 12 small cakes. (The recipe can be made up to this point in advance and refrigerated for up to a day.)

4. Heat some of the oil in a frying pan over a high heat. Cover the cakes with crumbs and fry until golden. Place on paper towels to drain, and then on a warm platter.

5. Mix the chopped cucumber, yogurt and lemon. Place in a bowl on the side of the dish of rice cakes. Serve with a mint leaf on top of each cake.

Wild Rice

Native Americans in the Northwest gathered wild rice in lakes. Always give wild rice extra time – it needs to be fully cooked and to grow in size to about six times what you started with.

Wild Rice Salad

This is just as good on a summer picnic as it is a wintry side dish.
It's filling and delightful.

Serves 6

4 cups water
¾ cup wild rice
1 teaspoon salt and black
    pepper to taste
1 small red onion, chopped
3 sticks celery, chopped finely
1 cup water chestnuts,
    drained and chopped
1 small apple, cored and
    chopped
⅔ cup olive oil
⅓ cup raspberry vinegar
½ cup fresh flat-leaf parsley,
    chopped
6oz fresh raspberries

1. Bring water to the boil and add the rice; return to a rolling boil and then reduce the heat to a simmer and cover tightly. After 30 minutes, add salt and pepper.

2. When the rice is cooked and while still hot, add the vegetables and apple. Taste and add salt and pepper.

3. Mix the olive oil and vinegar together with the parsley and combine with the rice and vegetables. Place in a large serving dish and serve warm or chilled. Sprinkle with rasbberries at the last minute.

Cooking Wild Rice

Disregard the directions on packets of wild rice. They tell you to cook for 30–40 minutes, when it can take more like 90 minutes for it to swell and soften. When cooking, just keep adding liquid if the rice dries out, and keep simmering until it 'blooms' or the grains open up.

Wild, Wild Rice and Mushroom Soup

Makes 6 cups

3 tablespoons butter
2 cloves garlic, chopped
1 cup finely chopped sweet
    onion such as Vidalia
10 each: shiitake, morel,
    porcini, and oyster
    mushrooms, chopped
2 tablespoons maize flour or
    cornflour
5 cups low-salt beef stock,
    heated
2 cups cooked wild rice
1 cup double cream
Salt and pepper to taste
½ cup dry sherry
6 fresh sage leaves

Try this in the autumn – it will make you feel so good inside.
It can be an elegant first course for company, or served with
gluten-free bread and a salad as a light supper.

1. Melt the butter and add the garlic and onion. Sauté for 5 minutes and add the mushrooms. Add the flour and stir until thickened, cooking for another 5 minutes.

2. Slowly stir in the stock, stirring constantly. Mix in the wild rice. Add the cream, salt and pepper.

3. Add the sherry and serve in heated bowls, with a sage leaf floating in each one.

Wild Rice Stuffing for Poultry

Makes enough stuffing for a 12lb turkey

4oz butter
1 large onion, chopped
3 sticks celery with their tops,
    chopped
1 teaspoon each: dried
    thyme, dried rosemary,
    dried sage, salt and
    pepper
1 cup walnut halves, toasted
    and chopped
3 tart apples, peeled, cored
    and chopped
½ cup dry white wine
½ cup fresh parsley, chopped
6 cups cooked wild rice

This can be baked inside the bird or in a separate casserole dish.
Allow about ¾ cup stuffing per pound of bird.

1. Melt the butter and add the onion, celery, herbs, salt and pepper. Sauté until softened, about 5 minutes. Add the walnuts and apples.

2. Mix all the ingredients in a large bowl, tossing with the wild rice until well combined.

3. Either stuff the mixture into a turkey or spoon it into a casserole dish and bake at 180°C/350°F/Gas 4 for 30 minutes, covered with aluminium foil.

Beef-Flavoured White Rice with Asian Spices

This is really good with any Asian-style stir-fry or any grilled meat or fish. Five-spice powder is available at some supermarkets and Asian markets.

Mix together all the ingredients except the rice to make a sauce. Boil to reduce for 3 minutes. Then mix in the rice, and serve hot.

Serves 4

½ cup soy sauce
¼ cup dry white wine or sake
1 tablespoon freshly grated ginger
1 tablespoon sesame seed oil
1 teaspoon five-spice powder
2 cloves garlic, chopped
4 spring onions, chopped
⅔ cup beef stock
3 cups hot cooked white rice

A Grass, Not a Rice

Wild rice is not really rice at all, but a grass. Wild rice (Zizania aquatica) is really an annual aquatic plant found mostly in the upper freshwater lakes of North America. It was used by tribes such as the Algonquin and Ojibwa as an important food source, and was a staple in their ritual harvest feasts. Stores of wild rice nourished them during the long winters.

Moroccan Hot and Tasty White Rice

Harissa is a classic Moroccan chilli paste. You can substitute quinoa, an ancient Aztec grain that is also gluten-free, for the rice in this dish.

1. Bring the water to the boil and add the salt and rice. Reduce the heat, cover, and cook until the rice is tender, about 25 minutes.

2. Sauté the garlic and onion in the olive oil over a low heat.

3. Add the remaining ingredients (including the parsley), and simmer, stirring occasionally, for 10 minutes.

4. When the rice is done, mix with the sauce and serve.

Serves 4

3 cups water
2 teaspoons salt
1 cup white rice
2 cloves garlic, finely chopped
1 onion, finely chopped
½ cup olive oil
6 dried apricots, quartered and soaked in ⅔ cup warm water
1 teaspoon harissa, or more if you like it really hot
1 teaspoon dried thyme
Salt to taste
½ cup parsley or coriander, chopped

Spanish-Style Rice

Serves 4

3 cups water
2 teaspoons salt
1 cup white rice
½ cup olive oil
1 large onion, chopped
1 clove garlic, chopped
2 jalapeño or poblano
    chillies, cored, seeded and
    chopped
1 roasted red pepper, from a
    jar or your own, chopped
4 ripe plum tomatoes, cored
    and chopped
1 teaspoon lemon zest
10 black olives, sliced
Freshly ground black pepper
    to taste

This is an excellent side dish with a great steak. It can be made in advance and then reheated just before serving.

1. Bring the water to the boil and add the salt and the rice. Reduce the heat to a simmer, cover, and cook until tender, about 25 minutes.

2. While the rice is cooking, heat the oil in a large frying pan.

3. Add the onion, garlic and chillies. Sauté over a low flame for 8–10 minutes.

4. Mix in the rest of the ingredients and simmer for 10 minutes.

5. Add to the hot rice and serve.

Ground Pepper

You can get pink, white and black peppercorns. Some cooks like to mix them. Some say there is a taste difference among the three. Other cooks use white pepper in white food so you won't see the black specks. Try a coarsely ground pepper in recipes like the one above. To coarse-grind, place 6 to 8 peppercorns between two pieces of greaseproof paper. Use a heavy frying pan to press down on the corns until they are cracked and in coarse pieces. Don't just lay them on a board and hit them with the pan or they will fly all over the kitchen.

Classic Italian Risotto

Risotto should be very creamy, with just a bit of toothsome resistance on the inside of each grain of rice.

1. Bring the stock to a slow simmer over a low heat and keep it hot.

2. Place the butter and oil in a heavy-bottomed pot, melt the butter, and add the onion, celery and celery leaves. Cook for 8–10 minutes.

3. Add the rice and stir to coat with butter and oil. Stir in the salt.

4. In ¼-cup increments, start adding the hot stock. Stir until the stock has been absorbed into the rice. Add another ¼ cup, stirring until all the stock is absorbed. Repeat this process until all the hot stock is gone. The risotto must be stirred constantly and takes about 35 minutes. (A stirring helper is nice.)

5. When all the stock is absorbed, taste the rice. If it needs more stock or water, add it and keep stirring. Add the cheese, parsley and pepper. Serve immediately.

Serves 4

5 cups bought or homemade chicken or vegetable stock
2 tablespoons butter
2 tablespoons olive oil
½ cup finely chopped sweet onion
2 sticks celery, finely chopped
¼ cup celery leaves, chopped
1½ cups Arborio rice
1 teaspoon salt, or to taste
⅔ cup freshly grated Parmesan cheese
¼ cup chopped parsley
Freshly ground black pepper to taste

Risotto with Radicchio and Gorgonzola Cheese

Serves 4

5 cups bought or homemade
   chicken, fish, or vegetable
   stock
2 tablespoons butter
2 tablespoons olive oil
½ cup finely chopped sweet
   onion
1 head radicchio, rinsed and
   chopped finely
1½ cups Arborio rice
Salt and freshly ground black
   pepper
¼ cup crumbled Gorgonzola
   cheese
Roasted red pepper strips
   and chopped parsley to
   garnish

This is very nicely pungent and good as a side dish with game or seafood.

1. Bring the stock to a slow simmer in a saucepan and keep it hot.

2. Heat the butter and oil in a large, heavy pan; add the onion and radicchio and sauté until softened, about 8 minutes. Add the rice and stir. Add salt and pepper.

3. Add the stock, ¼ cup at a time, until it is all absorbed, stirring constantly. This will take about 35 minutes. If the risotto is still not done, add water, ¼ cup at a time.

4. When the rice is done, stir in the Gorgonzola cheese and garnish with strips of roasted red pepper and parsley. Serve hot.

Flavouring with Bacon

Bacon is an excellent garnish. It can also add flavour to soups and stews, and fat for sautéing vegetables, mushrooms, and so on. A little goes a long way. If you are watching your diet, just drain the bacon well on paper towels and crumble it. Then sprinkle it on soups, salads, vegetables, pasta and rice.

Pumpkin and Bacon Risotto

This is a fine side dish in autumn and winter and makes a great accompaniment for turkey.

1. Put the diced pumpkin in a saucepan with water to cover and some salt. Simmer until the pumpkin is just tender, drain, and set aside, reserving the pumpkin liquid.

2. While the pumpkin is cooking, fry the bacon and drain it on paper towels. Crumble when cool. Heat the chicken stock in a large saucepan and keep at a low simmer.

3. Melt the butter in a big, heavy pot and add the onion; sauté until soft. Add the sage, oregano, rice, salt and pepper.

4. Slowly add the stock, ¼ cup at a time. When the pot hisses, add more stock, until it is all absorbed, and then, if still dry, add some of the pumpkin liquid.

5. Stir in the pumpkin, Parmesan cheese and bacon. Add extra pepper or butter if desired. Garnish with a sprinkle of roasted pumpkin seeds and serve immediately.

Serves 4

2 cups fresh pumpkin, peeled, seeded, and cut into dice
Water to cover the pumpkin
1 tablespoon salt
4 rashers streaky bacon
5 cups bought or homemade chicken stock
4 tablespoons butter
½ cup finely chopped sweet onion
2 teaspoons dried sage or 1 tablespoon chopped fresh
½ teaspoon dried oregano or 2 teaspoons chopped fresh
1½ cups Arborio rice
Salt and freshly ground black pepper
½ cup grated Parmesan cheese
¼ cup roasted pumpkin seeds, for garnish

Pumpkins Are Big in Vitamin A

To prepare fresh pumpkin for pies and soups, cut it in half, remove the seeds, and place it cut side down in a baking dish. Add ½in of water, cover with foil, and roast it for an hour or more in a low oven (120°C/250°F/Gas ½). Then it's easy to purée.

Baked Risotto with Seafood

Serves 6–8

1 small onion, chopped
3 tablespoons olive oil
1 tablespoon butter
Salt and pepper to taste
1 tablespoon fresh rosemary,
    crushed, or 2 teaspoons
    dried, broken up
1 teaspoon saffron threads
1 cup long-grain rice
2½ cups chicken stock
2 tablespoons Marsala or
    sherry wine
1lb raw prawns, peeled and
    deveined, or 1lb scallops
    or 1lb crabmeat

This is an old recipe. If you are having a dinner party and don't want to spend an hour making risotto, this works wonderfully well.

1. Preheat the oven to 180°C/350°F/Gas 4. Sauté the onion in the oil and butter until softened.

2. Add salt, pepper, rosemary, saffron and rice, and mix to cover the rice with the oil. Add the stock, cover tightly, and place in the oven.

3. After the rice has cooked for 10 minutes, add the Marsala or sherry. Return to the oven and cook for another 10 minutes.

4. Add the prawns or other seafood and continue to bake for 7 minutes more. Uncover and serve.

Instead of Seafood, Try ...

You can use prawns, scallops, crabmeat, lobster or crayfish in risotto. The trick is to use raw shellfish and put it in at the end of the cooking so it will not be overdone. By the same token, you can substitute 2 cups sliced mushrooms that have been sautéed separately in butter for the seafood.

Baked Mushroom and Fontina Risotto

You can add so many other ingredients – cut-up cooked chicken or turkey, chopped pears or apples, and your favourite herbs.

1. Preheat the oven to 180°C/350°F/Gas 4.

2. Heat the butter and olive oil in a flameproof casserole. Sauté the onion and garlic over a low flame until softened.

3. Add the salt, pepper, sage and rice; stir to coat. Add the stock and vermouth. Cover the rice and place in the oven.

4. After the rice has cooked for 20 minutes, sauté the mushrooms in the extra butter and stir into the rice. Re-cover the casserole and continue to cook for 15 minutes.

5. Just before serving, stir in the Fontina cheese.

Serves 6–8

1 tablespoon butter
3 tablespoons olive oil
1 small onion, chopped
2 garlic cloves, chopped
Salt and pepper to taste
6 large leaves fresh sage, ripped or cut up, or 2 teaspoons dried sage, crumbled
1 cup long-grain rice
2½ cups chicken stock
½ cup dry vermouth
8oz mixed mushrooms (shiitakes, porcinis, morels, chanterelles)
2 tablespoons butter
⅓ cup grated Fontina cheese

A Misunderstood Italian Staple

Many people think that risotto is simply rice that has been boiled with stock and herbs. But it's so much more – the technique is simple but demanding. The secret is the rice and how it's slow-cooked, using a bit of liquid until it's absorbed and then a bit more. It's been said that the rice will tell you when to add liquid – it hisses and sizzles, asking for the stock!

Chapter 10
Soups

Spicy Mexican Black Bean Soup

This traditional soup is easy but takes quite a while.
It freezes beautifully, so make a lot.

Makes about 6 pints

1lb ham hocks, split
1lb black beans, soaked in
    fresh water overnight
2 onions, chopped
4 cloves garlic, chopped
2 cups beef stock
Juice of 1 fresh lime
1 large (½lb) waxy potato,
    peeled and chopped
2 carrots, peeled and cut up
2 jalapeño chillies, cored,
    seeded and chopped
1 tablespoon ground cumin
1 tablespoon ground
    coriander
Salt and freshly ground black
    pepper to taste
½ cup chopped fresh flat-leaf
    parsley or coriander
1 cup golden rum
Sour cream and thinly sliced
    lemon or lime to garnish

1. Cover the ham hocks with cold water, bring to the boil, cover, and lower the heat to a simmer. Simmer for 4 hours or overnight. Cover the beans with cold water and soak overnight.

2. Remove the meat from the pot and reserve the cooking liquid. Remove the meat from the bones, discard the skin and bones, and chop the meat. Add the beans to the cooking liquid from the ham.

3. Stir the beef stock, lime juice, vegetables, spices, salt and pepper into the pot with the beans and cooking liquid. Add enough water to make 7 pints. Cover and simmer for 5 hours.

4. Stir in parsley or coriander, taste for seasonings, and add salt and pepper if necessary. Purée the soup in batches and return to the pot to heat. Return the meat to the pot.

5. Either add all of the rum at once and serve, or you can add it to individual bowls of soup. Top each bowl of soup with sour cream and a slice of lemon or lime.

Soaking Beans: The Long and Short of It

Our fast-food culture has moved the packagers of many varieties of dried beans to tell the consumer to boil, then soak for a short period of time. Sounds like a good idea; however, this method soon separates the bean from its skin and it just does not make for a good texture, whether you are leaving the beans whole or puréeing them. If you are short of time, use canned beans.

Onion Soup with Poached Eggs

When you come in from tobogganing or skiing, this brunch is about as good as it gets. Everything but the eggs can be made in advance.

∽

1. Fry the bacon until crisp and drain on paper towels; leave to cool, then crumble.

2. Sauté the onions in the olive oil, stir in the flour, and cook for a few minutes. Add the stock, wine, thyme and Worcestershire sauce. Cover and simmer for 1 hour. Taste for salt and pepper.

3. Just before serving, increase the heat. Swirl the soup and add the eggs, one at a time. Remove the eggs after 1 minute. Ladle soup and 1 egg each into four warm bowls and garnish with parsley and bacon.

Serves 4

4 rashers streaky bacon
2 Vidalia onions, sliced thinly
2 red onions, sliced thinly
2 yellow onions, sliced thinly
4 tablespoons olive oil or
    unsalted butter
1 tablespoon chickpea flour
4 cups low-salt beef stock
¼ cup dry red wine
1 tablespoon thyme
1 tablespoon Worcestershire
    sauce
Salt and pepper to taste
4 eggs
¼ cup chopped fresh parsley

Carrot, Cauliflower, and Caraway Soup

*This simple soup is full of intriguing flavours,
delicious as a first course or followed by a salad for lunch.*

∽

1. Boil the cauliflower and carrots in the stock with caraway seeds, lemon juice, orange zest, salt and pepper.

2. When tender, about 15–20 minutes, cool and then purée in a food processor or blender until smooth. Taste for salt and pepper, add cream.

3. Reheat but do not boil. Serve, garnished with the herbs.

Serves 4–6

1lb cauliflower florets
1lb carrots, peeled and cut
    into 1in pieces
4 cups chicken stock
1 teaspoon caraway seeds
Juice of ½ lemon
1 tablespoon finely grated
    orange zest
Salt and pepper to taste
1 cup double cream
½ cup chopped fresh parsley,
    for garnish
½ cup snipped fresh chives,
    for garnish

Thick and Rich Cream of Broccoli Soup

Serves 4–6

1lb broccoli
1 tablespoon olive oil or
    butter
1 large sweet onion, chopped
2 cloves garlic, chopped
2 tablespoons cornflour
    dissolved in 1/3 cup cold
    water
3 cups low-salt chicken stock
½ cup dry white wine
¼ teaspoon freshly grated
    nutmeg
Juice and rind of 1 lemon
Salt and freshly ground
    pepper to taste
1 cup double cream
¾ cup chopped prosciutto or
    other smoked ham

This soup can be served in small cups as a first course, or in bowls as a hearty lunch or supper. Garnish with a few small prawns floated on the top.

1. Wash, trim, and coarsely chop the broccoli; set aside in a colander to drain.

2. In a large soup pot, heat the oil or butter and add the onion and garlic. Sauté until softened. Stir in the cornflour and liquid ingredients. Mix in the broccoli, nutmeg, the lemon juice and rind, salt and pepper.

3. Simmer the soup, covered, until the broccoli is tender, about 15 minutes. Remove the lemon rind. Purée in batches. Stir in the cream and ham. Reheat but do not boil. Serve hot.

Adding Depth of Flavour to Soup

Adding sausage, ham or bacon to a soup enriches the flavour. The salt and smoke in the curing process of pork plus the herbs and spices used in sausage also add to the flavour of a soup or stew. Smoked ham hocks are a classical tasty touch in the cooking of the American South. They are inexpensive and meaty, but the skin and bones must be removed before the soup is served.

Old Southern Brunswick Stew

This traditional dish was originally made with local game. Don't remove the cloves – some families consider it good luck to find a clove in their bowl.

1. Dredge the chicken in the rice flour. In a large soup pot, brown the chicken in butter, add the water, cover, and simmer over a low heat for 20 minutes. Remove the chicken from the pot; when cool enough to handle, take the meat from the bones. Discard the bones.

2. While the chicken is cooling, stir the tomatoes and vegetables, cloves and Worcestershire sauce into the pot and cook for another 15 minutes, until tender.

3. Return the chicken meat to the pot and simmer for another 5 minutes. Season with salt and pepper. Serve with rice or mashed potatoes.

Serves 6

1 large chicken (4–5lb),
   cut into portions
⅓ cup rice flour
2 tablespoons butter
1 cup water
2 cups chopped tomatoes,
   fresh or canned
1 onion, chopped
1 cup butter beans
1 cup sweetcorn kernels
4 whole cloves
1 tablespoon Worcestershire
   sauce
Salt and pepper to taste

Kitchen Sink Soup

According to the old wives' tale, when asked, 'What's in the soup?' the cook would say, 'Everything but the kitchen sink!' And so it goes today – a frugal cook uses leftover veggies, stews and whatever is around to add to a soup base. Adding some canned beans and stock to a leftover stew can produce a hearty and nourishing main course.

Harvest Corn Chowder with Bacon

½lb bacon
2 large sweet onions,
    chopped finely
2 large potatoes, peeled
    and chopped
1 red pepper, cored, seeded
    and chopped
3 tablespoons cornflour
    mixed with ¼ cup water
    until smooth
2 pints homemade or bought
    low-salt chicken stock
3 cups fresh sweetcorn
    removed from cob
1 tablespoon salsa
1 cup whole milk
1 cup double cream
Salt and pepper to taste
¼ teaspoon ground nutmeg
1 bunch fresh parsley, stems
    removed, chopped

Use fresh ears of sweetcorn – with their tiny kernels, they are unbelievably sweet and tender. Frozen or canned corn just won't taste the same in this soup.

1. Fry the bacon until crisp and drain on paper towels; when cool, crumble and set aside, leaving the fat in the pan. Sauté the onions, potatoes, and pepper in the bacon fat for 10 minutes, stirring often.

2. Add the cornflour/water mixture and, stirring constantly, ladle in the chicken stock. Bring to the boil. Cover, lower the heat, and simmer for 30 minutes.

3. Stir in the rest of the ingredients. Taste, and season with salt and pepper. Do not boil after adding the cream. Serve hot, sprinkling the crumbled bacon over the top.

Summer Cucumber Soup

*This is so refreshing on a hot day. With few ingredients,
you can make an elegant and delightful summer soup.*

Mix all the ingredients in a ceramic or porcelain bowl. Chill overnight.
Serve in chilled bowls.

Serves 4

2 cucumbers, peeled and
    chopped
2 cups buttermilk
1 cup sour cream
2 teaspoons salt
Juice of 1 lemon
Grated rind of ½ lemon
⅔ tablespoon snipped
    fresh dill
½ cup snipped fresh chives
Freshly ground pepper
    to taste

Oyster Stew à la Grand Central Oyster Bar

*Here's a chance to replicate the cooking at New York City's Oyster Bar,
a legendary restaurant located in Grand Central Terminal.*

1. Mix 2 tablespoons butter, Worcestershire sauce, and fish stock together
   in a saucepan over medium heat. Whisk in the cornflour/water mixture.
   Add the cayenne, oysters, milk and double cream.

2. Heat carefully over a low flame until quite thick, stirring frequently
   for about 10 minutes. Just before serving, sprinkle with celery salt and
   paprika, then float a pat of butter on top of each bowl. Serve with salty
   crackers on the side.

Serves 4

2 tablespoons unsalted butter
2 tablespoons Worcestershire
    sauce
1 cup bottled or fresh fish
    stock
2 tablespoons cornflour
    mixed with 3 tablespoons
    cold water
⅛ teaspoon cayenne pepper
1 quart shucked oysters,
    drained
2 cups milk
1 cup double cream
Sprinkle of celery salt and
    paprika
4 pats butter
Salty crackers

Fresh Spring Soup with Baby Peas

Serves 4

1 cup chopped spring onions
2 cloves garlic, smashed
1 bunch sorrel (or 1 bunch
    watercress)
10 young dandelion leaves
    (small leaves only)
¼ cup olive oil
2oz cornflour
3 cups vegetable stock
⅛ teaspoon ground allspice
Zest of ½ lemon, grated
1½ cups fresh or frozen
    petit pois
1 cup double cream
Salt and pepper to taste

To vary the recipe, mix petit pois with chopped sugar snaps. Garnish with a few cooked prawns or a few tablespoons smoked ham, finely chopped.

1. Sauté the spring onions, the garlic and the dandelion leaves in olive oil for 5 minutes, to wilt them.

2. Whisk in the cornflour and vegetable stock. Stir in the allspice and lemon zest. When smooth, purée in the blender. Return the soup to the pot and add the peas. Cook for 5–8 minutes, or until tender.

3. Add the cream, salt and pepper. Do not boil, but serve hot.

Springtime, Anytime!

You can enjoy spring flavours at any time of year, thanks to fresh herbs and spring onions, both available all year round, and frozen petit pois.

Fresh Tuscan Tomato and Basil Soup

This taste is so fresh and delightful, you will want to serve it year-round.

Serves 4

4 tablespoons butter
¼ cup cornflour
2 cups cherry or grape
    tomatoes
2 cups fresh basil leaves,
    stems removed
2 tablespoons fresh oregano
    leaves
1½ cups milk
1 cup cream
Salt and pepper to taste

1. Make a roux with the butter and cornflour; cook over a medium heat for 5 minutes. Whizz the tomatoes, basil and oregano in the blender until smooth. Stir the tomatoes into the hot butter mixture.

2. Bring to the boil and add the milk and cream. Heat over a low flame and sprinkle with salt and pepper to taste.

Do Not Boil

When a recipe calls for cream, it's important to heat without boiling. If you boil it, you may get curdled soup. If it does get away from you, add a few tablespoons of boiling water and blend until the curds come back together.

Yellow Courgette and Apple Soup

A refreshing summer soup with loads of flavour.
Make a lot and serve it the next day to beat the heat.

Serves 4

2 shallots, chopped
1 Granny Smith apple, peeled,
    cored and chopped
2 medium yellow courgettes,
    chopped
4 tablespoons butter
3 cups fresh orange juice
1 cup apple juice
Juice of 1 fresh lime
¼ teaspoon ground cumin
⅛ teaspoon ground nutmeg
Salt and freshly ground white
    pepper to taste
4 tablespoons sour cream

In a large pot, sauté the shallots, apples and courgettes in the butter. Then add all the rest of the ingredients except the sour cream. Purée the soup, bring to the boil, and serve hot or cold. Garnish with sour cream.

Rhode Island Clam Chowder

Serves 4

2 dozen cherrystone clams
    (2in across)
3oz salt pork, chopped finely
1 large onion, chopped
1 carrot, peeled and chopped
2 sticks celery with tops,
    chopped fine
2 large potatoes, peeled
    and chopped
1 tablespoon cornflour (more
    if you like it really thick)
2 bay leaves
1 teaspoon dried thyme
1 teaspoon celery salt
1 tablespoon Worcestershire
    sauce
3 cups fish stock
Freshly ground black pepper
    to taste
½ cup chopped fresh parsley
    for garnish

This recipe is very traditional. Many cooks now substitute bacon for salt pork, but it's better to make it the traditional way.

1. Scrub the clams and place them in a large pot. Add 2 cups water, cover, and boil until the clams open. Remove them to a large bowl and leave to cool; reserve the juice. When cool, remove the clams, discard the shells, and chop the clams in a food processor.

2. In a large pot, fry the salt pork until crisp. Drain on paper towels. Add the vegetables to the pot and sauté until soft, about 10 minutes over medium heat. Blend in the cornflour and cook for 2 more minutes, stirring.

3. Add the reserved clam juice and the bay leaves, thyme, and celery salt to the pot. Stir in the Worcestershire sauce, clam broth, the chopped clams and the salt pork. Cover and simmer for 30 minutes. Before serving remove the bay leaf. Add black pepper to taste, garnish with chopped fresh parsley and serve hot.

Is That Clam Alive or Dead?

Never eat a dead clam. Always run them under cold water and scrub vigorously with a brush. To test for life, tap two clams together. You should hear a sharp click, not a hollow thud. If the clam sounds hollow, tap it again, and then, if still hollow-sounding, discard it.

Manhattan Red Clam Chowder

You can transform Rhode Island Clam Chowder to Manhattan with the addition of some tomatoes. This is so easy and good.

৩৩

After you have added all the ingredients for Rhode Island Chowder, add the tomatoes. Cover and simmer for 30 minutes. Serve hot. Garnish with chopped parsley.

Tomato or Cream in Your Clam Chowder?

Manhattan clam chowder, made with tomatoes, is a latecomer to the chowder arena. During the eighteenth and nineteenth centuries, tomato-based chowder was banned in New England. In fact, tomatoes were suspect for many years – it was the invention and distribution of catsup in the early twentieth century that brought the tomato into its own in America.

New England Clam Chowder

To the basic Rhode Island Clam Chowder, you simply add cream and/or milk to transform a clear chowder into a rich and creamy one.

৩৩

Bring the chowder base to a slow boil before adding the milk and cream. Reduce the heat to simmer and cover to let the ingredients marry. After you add the milk and cream, do not boil. If you do, your soup is likely to curdle. Taste and adjust the seasonings, if necessary. Garnish with freshly chopped parsley.

Serves 6

1 recipe Rhode Island Clam
    Chowder (see page 142)
2 14oz cans chopped
    tomatoes with their juice
Parsley, chopped, for garnish

Serves 4–6

1 recipe Rhode Island Clam
    Chowder (see page 142),
    with an extra tablespoon
    cornflour added for a
    thicker consistency
1 cup whole milk
1 cup cream
Parsley, chopped, for garnish

Indian Mulligatawny Soup

Serves 4–6

*This is a staple in India and best made a day in advance.
You may have to thin it with more water or stock if it gets too thick.*

1 large sweet onion, such as
  Vidalia, chopped
4 cloves garlic, chopped
2 tablespoons chopped fresh
  ginger
1 hot chilli, serrano or
  poblano, cored, seeded
  and chopped
½ cup unsalted butter
1½ tablespoons Madras curry
  powder, or more to taste
¼ cup rice flour
10 cups chicken stock
2 cups red lentils
1 14oz can unsweetened
  coconut milk
Salt and freshly ground black
  pepper to taste
6 sprigs fresh coriander leaves
  for garnish
Lemon slices for garnish

1. Sauté the onions, garlic, ginger and pepper in the butter over a medium heat until soft.

2. Blend in the curry powder and rice flour. Cook for 4 minutes; add the chicken stock and lentils, mixing thoroughly. Simmer, covered, for 1 hour or until the lentils are very tender.

3. Cool and then purée in the blender. Add the coconut milk, salt and pepper and reheat. Garnish with coriander sprigs and slices of fresh lemon.

Healthy Soup

The healing qualities of chicken soup plus the healthful properties of Indian herbs and spices make this a very nourishing soup. The name means 'pepper water.'

Delicious Dumplings for Soup

Dumplings are fun and delicious. They add body to soups and stews.

෨෨

Mix all the ingredients together and work into a stiff dough. Drop by the teaspoonful into any soup you are preparing and cook for 2–3 minutes before serving.

Serves 4

5 tablespoons potato flour
1 teaspoon baking powder
1 tablespoon milk
1 egg, beaten
1 teaspoon dried chives or oregano or ⅛ teaspoon nutmeg
½ teaspoon ground black pepper

Puffy Potato Dumplings

These give a satisfying finish to a thick soup or rich stew.
Riced potatoes work better than mashed for this.

෨෨

1. Mix the milk, baking powder, pepper, salt and whole egg into the potatoes.

2. Gently fold in the egg whites. Preheat the grill. Drop the mixture by tablespoonfuls into a stew. Leave to simmer for 3–4 minutes. Place the dish under the grill until delicately browned.

Serves 4

3oz milk or cream
1 teaspoon baking powder
½ teaspoon ground white or black pepper
½ teaspoon salt
1 whole egg, beaten
1 cup riced or mashed potatoes
2 egg whites, stiffly beaten

Prawn Bisque with Scallops

Serves 4–6

2 chopped shallots
2 tablespoons butter
2 tablespoons cornflour
1 tablespoon tomato paste
4 cups Prawn Shell Stock (see page 149) or bottled fish stock
½lb raw prawns, cleaned and deveined
½lb scallops
1 cup double cream
Salt and pepper to taste
1 tablespoon dry sherry per bowl of soup
Chopped parsley for garnish

This is an elegant first course or a delicious lunch. It's very easy to make in advance, adding the cream at the last minute when reheating.

1. Sauté the shallots in the butter. Blend in the cornflour and tomato paste. Add the stock and bring to the boil. Simmer for 10 minutes.

2. Spoon in the prawns and scallops. Leave to cool. Blend in batches until puréed. Return to the pot and add the cream. Taste for salt and pepper, adding as necessary.

3. Spoon in the sherry. Garnish with parsley.

Italian Sausage, Bean and Vegetable Soup

Serves 4–6

1lb dry-cured sausage, cut into 1in pieces
1 large red onion, chopped
4 cloves garlic, chopped
¼ cup olive oil
2 14oz cans chopped tomatoes with their juice
Bunch escarole, washed, base stems removed, chopped
1½ pints beef stock
2 14oz cans cannellini or borlotti beans
1 tablespoon dried oregano
1 cup grated Parmesan cheese

There's nothing like a bowl of good soup, especially when you are in a hurry. This one is quite quickly made and will make you feel warm inside.

1. Sauté the sausage, onion, and garlic in the olive oil.

2. When the onion and garlic are soft, add the rest of the ingredients, except the Parmesan cheese. Cover and simmer over very low heat for 30 minutes. Garnish with Parmesan cheese and serve.

Chapter 11
Asian Dishes

Asian-Style Soup with Rice Noodles

Serves 4

1 quart chicken stock
2 cloves garlic, chopped
1in fresh ginger, peeled
     and chopped
1 bunch spring onions,
     thinly sliced
12 canned water chestnuts
1 cup bean sprouts
½ cup dry sherry
½ cup soy sauce
½lb soft tofu
2 cups rice noodles, cooked
12 mange-tout, sliced on the
     diagonal, for garnish

This can be served in small bowls as a first course or in large bowls for lunch. The contrast between soft and crunchy, spicy and sweet, makes it interesting.

1. Bring the chicken stock to the boil and add all but the tofu, noodles and mange-tout. Cover and simmer for 10 minutes. Add the tofu.

2. Stir gently and add the cooked noodles. Garnish with the mange-tout and serve.

Soy Galore

Tofu is made of soy and is related to all soy products, such as soy sauce, soy nuts and soy paste. All are excellent food supplements. Tofu is available soft and firm. The firm version is excellent fried. The more tofu you eat, the better off your arteries will be – it has no cholesterol.

Prawn and Coconut Soup

This is equally good served chilled or hot. You can add a cup of cooked rice to this, but it is not necessary.

1. Sauté the shallots in the oil until soft, about 10 minutes over a medium heat. Stir in the cornflour and cook until very thick.

2. Add the liquid ingredients and cook, covered, over a very low heat for 30 minutes.

3. Stir in the rice and prawns; heat until the prawns turn pink. Add salt and white pepper to taste and serve hot or cold.

Prawn Shell Stock

Stock made from shellfish shells makes a flavourful addition to seafood soup. Next time you are preparing prawns, reserve the shells. Add 1 cup of water, 1 cup of wine and a bay leaf to the shells from a pound of prawns. Bring to the boil, lower the heat and simmer, covered, for 20 minutes. Strain and use as stock for soup.

Serves 4

2 shallots, chopped
2 teaspoons groundnut oil or other vegetable oil
2 tablespoons cornflour
1½ cups Prawn Shell Stock (this page), warmed
½ cup dry white wine
1 cup unsweetened coconut milk
1 cup cooked rice (optional)
1lb raw prawns, shelled and deveined, chopped
Salt and freshly ground white pepper to taste

Spinach Soup with Puffy Dumplings

Serves 4

3 pints chicken stock
8oz fresh baby spinach, shredded, or 10oz frozen spinach, thawed and squeezed to remove moisture
¼ cup fresh lemon juice
¼ cup dry white wine
¼ cup soy sauce
1 teaspoon sugar
1 teaspoon Thai green chilli paste, or to taste
¼ teaspoon ground coriander
Grated rind of ½ lemon for garnish
1 recipe Puffy Dumplings (this page)

You can add other shredded vegetables to this soup, such as watercress, Chinese cabbage or mange-tout.

Bring the chicken stock to the boil and add the shredded spinach. Simmer for 10 minutes and add the rest of the ingredients, except the dumplings. Float the dumplings on top of the soup. Cover and cook for 2 minutes, turning the dumplings after 2 minutes.

Garnishes Transform Simple Soups

If your soup seems a bit dull, try adding seasoned salt or floating fresh herbs such as chives, oregano or parsley on top. Tasty crackers can be added to the soup too, as well as various kinds of cheese.

Puffy Dumplings

Serves 4

¼ cup rice flour
1 teaspoon baking powder
½ teaspoon black pepper, or to taste
1 teaspoon chopped chives
4–5 teaspoons milk
1 egg, beaten

These can be used in any soup you like – not only in Asian recipes, but also in Mediterranean vegetable soups and even in Hungarian goulash.

Mix the dry ingredients in a bowl; stir in the milk and egg until a stiff dough is formed. Drop by half-teaspoonfuls into hot soup. Stir gently so that the dumplings cook evenly.

Rice Flour Crêpes

Use milk instead of water in this recipe if you want a richer crêpe.

1. Place the eggs, water and salt in a blender. Add pepper and flour and blend, stopping once to scrape the sides of the goblet.

2. Oil a nonstick pan, set it over a medium heat, and slowly pour or ladle a small amount of the batter into the pan, lifting and tipping to spread the batter.

3. When the edges start to brown, flip the crêpe. Cook for only a minute on the second side or it will become crisp and not pliable.

4. Cool and stack between sheets of greaseproof paper.

Crêpes, Pancakes, Tortillas and Cannelloni – Ripe for the Stuffing

While gluten-free flours can be a disaster under certain circumstances, they are a great success when it comes to crêpes, pancakes and corn tortillas, which are made like crêpes. You can stuff them like wontons, make tubes and fill them, or fold them and dip them into a spicy sauce. Experiment.

Serves 4

2 eggs
1½ cups water or milk
½ teaspoon salt
¼ teaspoon freshly ground white pepper
1 cup rice flour
Groundnut or canola oil

Stir-Fried Prawns
and Vegetables in Rice Crêpe Wraps

Serves 4

1 tablespoon sesame seed oil
¼ cup groundnut oil
4 spring onions
4 garlic cloves, chopped
1 courgette, finely chopped
1 onion, finely chopped
⅔lb raw prawns, shelled and
 deveined
½ cup almonds, chopped
1 tablespoon Thai fish sauce
¼ cup dry sherry
2 teaspoons wasabi paste
1 recipe for Rice Flour Crêpes
 (see page 151)
1 egg, beaten

*These are great stuffed or stacked with filling between the layers.
Or try dipping them in teriyaki sauce.*

1. Heat the sesame and groundnut oil in a wok or frying pan and add the vegetables and prawns. Stir and cook until the prawns turn pink. Add the rest of the ingredients except for the crêpes and the egg. Mix until well sauced.

2. Place the prawns and vegetables in a bowl and cool. Put a spoonful of filling on one half of a crêpe. Paint the rim of the circle with the beaten egg. Fold over and press to seal.

3. Grill on a high heat or steam the filled crêpes for 10 minutes or until they are steaming hot. Serve hot.

Spicy Beef-Stuffed Mushrooms

Serves 4

½lb beef sirloin, chopped
½ cup chopped onion
2 cloves garlic, chopped
1in fresh ginger, peeled and
 chopped
2 tablespoons cooking oil
1 tablespoon Worcestershire
 sauce
1 egg, slightly beaten
Salt and freshly ground black
 pepper to taste
12–16 large mushroom caps,
 stems removed

*The mushrooms should be about 2½in across. This is a great side dish or
appetizer. Served with salad leaves, stuffed mushrooms make a fine lunch.*

1. Sauté the meat, onion, garlic and ginger in the oil, mixing constantly to break up lumps. When the meat turns pink (but not grey or brown), remove from the heat and add the Worcestershire sauce, taste and add salt and pepper. When almost cool, blend in the egg.

2. Preheat the oven to 180°C/350°F/Gas 4. Divide the stuffing between the mushrooms in a baking dish. Pour in water to a depth of ¼in around the mushrooms.

3. Bake the mushrooms for 25 minutes. You can sprinkle them with chopped fresh herbs of your choice when done.

Peanut Dipping Sauce for Satay

This is excellent with chicken, beef, pork or lamb. It can be made in advance and reheated at the last minute.

Makes about 2 cups (enough for 12 skewers of meat)

½ cup unsweetened coconut milk
1 cup dry roasted peanuts
1 tablespoon lemon or lime juice
1 tablespoon dark brown sugar, or more to taste
1 tablespoon dark soy sauce
½ teaspoon chilli oil, or to taste
2 tablespoons groundnut oil
2 tablespoons finely chopped sweet onion
2 cloves garlic, chopped

1. In a food processor, whizz the coconut milk, peanuts, lemon or lime juice, brown sugar, soy sauce and chilli oil. Process until very smooth.

2. Heat the groundnut oil in a large saucepan. Add the onion and garlic and cook over a medium heat until just soft, about 3 minutes.

3. Pour the peanut mixture into the pan and mix well. Heat on low, but do not boil.

Wooden Skewers Must Be Soaked!

Wooden skewers must be soaked or they will burn when on the barbecue or under the grill. Place them in a pan of water for an hour. You can also get very fancy skewers with decorative handles or metal at the ends. Simple metal skewers are also available. When using metal skewers, be sure to oil them to keep the food from sticking.

Thai Chicken with Peanut Dipping Sauce

The chicken or other meat for satay should be grilled over hot coals. You can use tender beef instead of chicken. The marinade is good with any meat.

Serves 4

1½lb boneless, skinless
   chicken breast
½ cup soy sauce
2 teaspoons Thai red chilli
   paste, or to taste
2 tablespoons chopped fresh
   ginger
1 tablespoon sesame oil
2 tablespoons dry sherry

1. Set twelve 10in skewers to soak in water to cover for at least 40 minutes and rinse the chicken. Pat the chicken dry and cut it into bite-sized pieces.

2. Mix the rest of the ingredients together and add the chicken. Cover and marinate for 2 hours.

3. String the chicken on the skewers and grill over glowing coals for 4–5 minutes on each side. Serve with any of the dipping sauces listed in this chapter.

Spicy Sesame Sauce for Lamb, Chicken or Falafel

Tahini, sesame-seed paste, is the basis of this delicious sauce. Use it as a dipping sauce for any meat, fish or shellfish.

Makes 1½ cups

1–2 cloves garlic, peeled
1 teaspoon salt, or to taste
½ cup tahini
¼ cup lemon juice
¼ cup water
¼ cup groundnut or olive oil
2 tablespoons chopped fresh
   parsley or coriander
¼ teaspoon ground cumin

Mash the garlic and salt together to make a paste. Add the rest of the ingredients and blend well. Store, covered, in the refrigerator.

Ginger and Spice Dipping Sauce

This is an all-purpose dipping sauce or marinade.

Mix all the ingredients together. Serve with just about anything.

Bits and Bites in Asian Cooking

One of the most delightful things about a great deal of Asian cooking is that you aren't stuck with an overloaded plate stacked with just one thing. In much the same way that Latin American cooking employs wraps, many Asian cuisines use lettuce and other leaves for wrapping food. This is a great way to enhance a gluten-free diet.

Makes 1½ cups

1 cup soy sauce
1 tablespoon chopped fresh
   ginger
1 tablespoon fresh lime juice
1 tablespoon concentrated
   pineapple juice
2 tablespoons gluten-free
   English mustard

Chinese-Style Crab in Red Chilli Sauce

Ever since Marco Polo took pasta to Italy, Italians and the rest of the world have loved it. This dish could have been one that old Polo loved.

1. Heat the oil in a large frying pan or wok.

2. Add the vegetables and stir-fry for 3 minutes. Then stir in the soy, tomatoes, crabmeat and wine.

3. Boil the noodles according to the directions on the pack, then add to the sauce and let the liquid soak in. Serve hot.

Serves 4

¼ cup groundnut oil
4 cloves garlic, chopped
1 bunch spring onions,
   chopped
2in fresh ginger, peeled and
   chopped
4–6 Scotch bonnet chillies,
   or to taste, cored, seeded
   and chopped
¼ cup dark soy sauce
2 fresh tomatoes, cored
   and chopped
1 cup crabmeat
½ cup dry white wine or
   rice wine
8oz medium rice noodles

Sesame-Crusted Chicken Breasts

Serves 4

¼ cup pineapple juice
¼ cup orange juice
1 tablespoon lime juice
½ cup soy sauce
1in fresh ginger, peeled and chopped
2 cloves garlic, or to taste, chopped
1 teaspoon chilli oil, or to taste
2 large boneless, skinless chicken breasts, halved
1 egg, beaten
½ cup sesame seeds

Serve this with rice and lots of vegetables. Leftovers can be chopped, mixed with a spicy sauce, and used to fill Rice Flour Crêpes (page 151) as a delicious snack.

1. In a ceramic or glass bowl large enough to hold the chicken, whisk together the juices, soy sauce, ginger, garlic and chilli oil. Rinse the chicken breasts and pat dry with paper towels. Add the chicken to the sauce and turn to coat. Cover and refrigerate for 4 hours.

2. Drain the chicken; dip in beaten egg and then in sesame seeds. Grill or sauté in oil for 6 minutes per side, depending on the thickness of the meat. Serve hot.

Chilli and Other Hot Sauces

Chinese, Indians and other groups in Asia, Southeast Asia and Asia Minor make their own versions of chilli for cooking. Chilli oil is extremely hot. Chilli paste comes in green and red variations and is popular in Thailand. The Chinese make a chilli and garlic paste called Sichuan chilli. Tabasco sauce, fresh chopped chillies (red and/or green), cayenne pepper and red chilli flakes can be substituted.

Roasted Poussins with Ginger-Orange Glaze

*This is simple to make and tastes wonderful. It makes
a delicious, but sticky, picnic.*

Serves 4

2 poussins, split
2 tablespoons olive oil
*Generous sprinkle of salt and
     pepper*
*1 tablespoon orange
     marmalade*
2 tablespoons groundnut oil
1 tablespoon soy sauce
2 tablespoons orange juice
*1 tablespoon chopped fresh
     ginger*

1. Preheat the oven to 190°C/375°F/Gas 5.

2. Rinse the birds, pat dry with paper towels, brush with olive oil and
    sprinkle with salt and pepper.

3. Stir the rest of the ingredients together in a small saucepan over a low
    heat to make the glaze; set aside.

4. Roast the birds in a baking dish, cut side up, for 15 minutes. Turn them
    and brush with the glaze. Continue to roast for another 20 minutes,
    brushing with the glaze every 5 minutes.

Fresh Ginger

*You can use fresh root ginger in all kinds of dishes, from dinners to desserts.
Dried ground ginger, ginger snaps and candied ginger are often used in
cooking. Unpeeled fresh ginger freezes beautifully and can be added to sauces,
salad dressings, and desserts. When you want to use it, cut off an inch or two
and peel it, then grate or chop it finely.*

Curried Prawns with Avocados

Serves 4

¾ cup mayonnaise

2 teaspoons curry powder

Juice of 1 lime

1 teaspoon hot chilli oil or
    hot pepper sauce such
    as Tabasco

½lb raw medium prawns,
    peeled and deveined

4 ripe avocados, halved,
    peeled, and pitted

Hungarian sweet or hot
    paprika to taste

Dry roasted peanuts, for
    garnish

*Adapting Asian flavours to Western lifestyles can produce
delightful dishes such as this. Quick and simply made,
it's a fine lunch or light supper served with rice.*

1. Preheat the oven to 180°C/350°F/Gas 4.

2. Mix the mayonnaise with the curry, lime juice and hot chilli oil. Chop the prawns and mix them with the mayonnaise sauce.

3. Place the avocado halves in an oiled baking dish. Spoon the prawns and sauce mixture into the avocados. Sprinkle with paprika and peanuts.

4. Bake the prawn-stuffed avocados for 20 minutes. You can vary this by adding chopped tart apple, pineapple or red grapes.

How Hot Is Too Hot?

Any supermarket has dozens of bottles of various kinds of hot sauce, from Jamaican to Chinese to African to, of course, Asian. The degrees of heat and other flavourings such as garlic and ginger vary. However, for the flavours of the food to come through, use only as much as you find adds piquancy – don't burn your tongue or you will kill valuable taste buds.

Curried Lamb Grilled on Skewers

Try grilling these and serving with Spicy Sesame Sauce (page 154).

1. Mix the first six ingredients together in a bowl. Add the lamb and turn to coat with the marinade. Cover and refrigerate for 2 hours.

2. Soak 8–10 wooden skewers for at least 40 minutes. Thread the pieces of lamb on the skewers and grill over hot coals for 4 minutes on each side. Serve hot.

Serves 4

½ cup groundnut oil
1 teaspoon curry powder
2 tablespoons lemon juice
4 cloves garlic, chopped
½ teaspoon ground coriander
2 teaspoons chilli sauce, or
 to taste
1lb lamb chunks, from the leg
 or shoulder, cut into bite-
 sized chunks

Lobster with Sherry Sauce

This adaptation is a unique way to serve lobster.
Garnish with fresh lemon wedges.

1. Boil the lobsters for 20 minutes, then split them and crack the claws.

2. Preheat the grill to its hottest setting.

3. Mix the rest of the ingredients together in a saucepan to make the sauce. Bring to the boil and spoon over the lobsters.

4. Grill for 3 minutes. Serve.

Serves 4–6

4 chicken lobsters,
 1–1¼lb each
1 teaspoon Chinese five-spice
 powder
1 clove garlic, chopped
¼ cup sesame seed oil
¼ cup sherry
Juice of ½ lemon
2 tablespoons chopped
 fresh ginger

Mange-Tout with Water Chestnuts and Ginger

Serves 4

1lb mange-tout, ends
    trimmed
½ cup groundnut oil
1 8oz can water chestnuts,
    drained, rinsed, and sliced
½ cup unsalted peanuts
2 tablespoons soy sauce
1 teaspoon lemon juice
1 tablespoon chopped fresh
    ginger
Tabasco or other red pepper
    sauce

This tasty side dish is very fast and good. It's a boon for the busy working person who wants fresh vegetables but has little time.

1. Place the mange-tout in a hot wok or frying pan with the oil. Stir to coat, then add the water chestnuts and peanuts, stirring again.

2. Continue cooking, and after 5 minutes, add the rest of the ingredients. Mix well and serve hot or at room temperature.

Cheese and Milk in Asian Cooking

The reason that cheese and milk are practically nonexistent in Asian cooking is that Asian countries do not have many dairy cows. In some areas, water buffalo work hard and produce milk too. Water buffalo in Italy provide the milk for a wonderful mozzarella cheese. Asians substitute tofu for meat, and what meat they do eat is stretched with vegetables and rice. Fish is popular in lake and seaside communities. Western cooks have adapted Asian flavours in popular fusion dishes.

Rich and Thick Chicken Curry with Peppers

*This is a British adaptation of an Indian curry. Serve with rice
(white or brown) and Major Grey's mango chutney.*

1. Sauté the garlic, onion and peppers in the groundnut oil. Dredge the chicken in rice flour, salt and pepper. Add to the vegetables and cook over a medium heat for 2 minutes per side, until just golden.

2. Stir in the mushrooms. Mix in the curry powder and cornflour. Add the warmed chicken stock and stir until smooth and very thick. Stir in the cream.

3. Cover and cook over a very low heat, being careful not to boil. Garnish the chicken with parsley or coriander and serve with rice and plenty of accompaniments.

Serves 4

2 cloves garlic, chopped
½ red onion, finely chopped
1 red pepper, cored, seeded
and finely chopped
1 green pepper, cored, seeded
and finely chopped
½ cup groundnut or olive oil
1lb skinless, boneless
chicken breasts, cut
into 8 portions
½ cup rice flour
1 tablespoon salt and ground
black pepper to taste
24 tiny button mushrooms,
stems trimmed
2 tablespoons Madras curry
powder
3 tablespoons cornflour
1 cup chicken stock, warmed
1 cup double cream
½ cup chopped parsley or
coriander
3 cups cooked white or
brown rice
Chopped fresh fruit, peanuts
and chutney
to accompany

Cold Cellophane Noodle Salad with Crabmeat

Cellophane noodles do not usually need to be cooked separately in lots of water. They are very thin and are made from mung bean flour.

Serves 4

6oz cellophane noodles, cooked according to package directions
2 tablespoons rice wine vinegar
½ cup groundnut oil
¼ cup light soy sauce
2 cloves garlic, chopped
Grated rind of 1 lemon
Juice of 1 lemon
2 cups shredded Chinese cabbage
1 long cucumber, peeled and julienned
1lb cooked crabmeat

Mix the vinegar, oil and soy sauce in a large salad bowl. Add the garlic and lemon rind, crabmeat and noodles. Mix well, toss in the rest of the ingredients, and serve.

Asian Noodles – Most Are Gluten-Free!

Take your glasses to an Asian supermarket and check the labels on the rice noodles. You'll find that almost all are made with rice, only rice, and not wheat flour. You can use these noodles in soups or in place of pasta. Also, we urge you to try spaghetti squash if you haven't already – it holds up well, is easy to prepare, and is delicious!

Chinese Cabbage with Sesame

Chinese cabbage is wonderful cooked or served raw in salads. It's pale green, mild, leafy and very good for you!

Serves 4

2 tablespoons sesame seed oil
2 tablespoons canola or other light oil
1 tablespoon sesame seeds
1 1½lb head Chinese cabbage, thinly sliced
Juice of ½ lemon
2 cloves garlic, chopped
Salt, pepper and soy sauce to taste

1. Place the oils in a hot wok or frying pan. Add the sesame seeds and toast for 2 minutes.

2. Stir in the cabbage, lemon juice and garlic. Toss until just wilted, about 4 minutes. Add the seasonings and serve.

Chapter 12
Corn-Based Dishes

Thick and Creamy Corn and Lima Bean Casserole

2 tablespoons unsalted butter

½ sweet onion, finely
    chopped

½ cup chopped celery

½ cup chopped celeriac

¼ cup red pepper, roasted
    and chopped

2 tablespoons maize flour
    (masa harina), potato
    flour or cornflour

½ cup rich chicken stock

10oz canned lima beans

10oz frozen sweetcorn

2 eggs, well beaten

1½ cups whipping cream

1 teaspoon salt

1 teaspoon sweet paprika

1 teaspoon ground black
    pepper

1 teaspoon ground coriander

½ teaspoon ground allspice

1 cup gluten-free
    breadcrumbs

1 cup grated Cheddar cheese

*This makes a satisfying meal and can be made with
chopped ham to add to the flavour and protein.*

1. Preheat the oven to 180°C/350°F/Gas 4. Melt the butter in a large cas-serole dish. Add the onion, celery, celeriac and red pepper; sauté over a low heat until soft, about 10 minutes.

2. Mix in the flour and stir, cooking gently for 3 minutes.

3. Add the chicken stock, lima beans and sweetcorn. Bring to the boil, and then lower the heat to a simmer and cook for about 20 minutes.

4. Take off the heat. Mix together the eggs and cream; blend quickly into the vegetables. Mix in the salt and spices. Sprinkle the top with bread-crumbs and cheese.

5. Bake until golden brown and bubbling. Serve hot.

Better Than Canned

Stay away from canned creamed sweetcorn and stick with fresh or frozen, making your own cream sauce. It's easy and gluten-free, and tastes so much better than the ones made with soups or mixes.

Old Maryland Corn and Crabmeat Pie

*You can cut the wedges as small as you like to make a wonderful appetizer,
or cut the pie into quarters for a lunch or supper dish.*

1. Preheat the oven to 180°C/350°F/Gas 4. In a saucepan, heat the butter and add the onion and carrot. Cook, stirring, until the onion and carrot are softened. Add the cornflour and mustard.

2. In a separate pan, warm the chicken stock and wine. Slowly add to the saucepan, stirring into the onion and carrot mixture. Stir until smooth and thickened. Simmer until the vegetables are tender.

3. Add all the other ingredients except the topping. Sprinkle with salt and pepper to taste and stir to mix. Place in a buttered pie dish and cover with pastry or mashed potatoes.

4. Place in the oven and bake for about 30 minutes.

**Serves 8 as a first course,
4–6 as a main course**

2 tablespoons butter
1 onion, chopped
1 carrot, chopped
2 tablespoons cornflour
½ teaspoon gluten-free
    English mustard
½ cup chicken stock
½ cup dry white wine
1 cup double cream
1 teaspoon Worcestershire
    sauce
10oz frozen sweetcorn
1lb crabmeat
½ teaspoon dried dill or
    1 teaspoon chopped fresh
⅛ teaspoon freshly grated
    nutmeg
Salt and pepper to taste
Pastry for a 10in pie or 2 cups
    mashed potatoes

Spicy Cornbread Stuffed with Chillies and Cheese

Serves 6–8

1 cup cornmeal

1 cup maize flour (masa
  harina) or rice flour

¼ cup light brown sugar

3 teaspoons gluten-free
  baking powder or
  bicarbonate of soda

1 teaspoon salt

1 teaspoon dried red chilli
  flakes, or to taste

½ cup buttermilk

½ cup sour cream

2 eggs, beaten

2 tablespoons unsalted
  butter, melted

½ cup chipotle chillies,
  chopped

½ cup grated Monterey jack
  or Cheddar cheese

*This is perfect with soup, fried chicken, stews and chowders.
Adding some refried beans to the stuffing is enough
to make it a fine brunch with eggs.*

1. Preheat the oven to 200°C/400°F/Gas 6. In a large bowl, mix together the cornmeal, flour, sugar, baking powder, salt and red chilli flakes.

2. Mix in the buttermilk, sour cream, eggs and melted butter.

3. Oil an 8in square tin. Place half the batter in the pan. Sprinkle with the chillies and cheese. Cover with the rest of the batter. Bake for 20–25 minutes.

The Word on Chipotle

Chipotle chillies are jalapeño chilli peppers that have been smoked and preserved in brine or vinegar. They are useful in cooking and baking, adding a smoky zing to recipes.

Winter Cranberry-Orange Cornbread

This is wonderful with turkey and can also be chopped and used as stuffing.

1. Preheat the oven to 200°C/400°F/Gas 6. Oil an 8in square tin.

2. In a large bowl, mix all the dry ingredients together. Slowly stir in the rest of the ingredients.

3. Turn into the tin and bake for 20–25 minutes. Cool for a few minutes before cutting into squares and serving.

Serves 8–10

1 cup cornmeal
1 cup maize flour (masa harina) or rice flour
¼ cup light brown sugar
3 teaspoons gluten-free baking powder or bicarbonate of soda
1 teaspoon salt
1 cup milk
2 eggs, beaten
3 tablespoons unsalted butter, melted
½ cup dried cranberries
Zest of 1 orange
½ cup chopped walnuts (optional)

Sweetcorn Soufflé

This is very good with roast turkey or pork. Just make sure the oven is very hot.
You can add chopped chillies or vary the herbs to change the flavour.

1. Preheat the oven to 190°C/375°F/Gas 5. Whizz the flour, milk, egg yolks, baking powder, cheese, salt, pepper and herbs in a food processor. Place in a bowl and add the sweetcorn.

2. Beat the egg whites until stiff and fold them into the mixture.

3. Grease a 4-pint soufflé dish. Pour the mixture into the dish, and place in the middle of the oven for 25–30 minutes, until brown and puffed. Serve hot.

Serves 4–6

½ cup maize flour (masa harina) or rice flour
¼ cup milk or single cream
3 eggs, separated
3 teaspoons gluten-free baking powder
2 tablespoons finely grated Parmesan cheese
Salt, pepper and 1 teaspoon of your favourite herbs, to taste
1 cup fresh sweetcorn, cut off the cob, or frozen

Mexican-Style Corn Tortillas Stuffed with Prawns and Avocado

Makes 6 tortillas

6 corn tortillas or 6 crêpes
24 raw king prawns, peeled and deveined
½ cup dry white wine
6 medium avocados, peeled and sliced
1 red onion, thinly sliced
Juice of 2 fresh limes
1 teaspoon freshly ground coriander seeds
1 tablespoon dried red chilli flakes
1 cup fresh or bottled salsa
1 cup sour cream
½ cup chopped coriander or parsley

*This is a fine lunch or brunch dish on a hot day,
very good with margaritas or Bloody Marys.*

1. Toast the tortillas or crêpes and place on serving plates.

2. Poach the cleaned prawns in the white wine and drain.

3. Stack 4 prawns on each tortilla, add the avocado and onion, and sprinkle with lime juice, coriander and chilli flakes.

4. Spoon salsa over each tortilla, add a dollop of sour cream, and garnish with either coriander or parsley.

The Right Flour

You can make regular corn tortillas – the only hard part is getting them to be thin and crisp as opposed to thick and hard to eat. Serious Latin American cooks buy a press to stamp out their tortillas. Or you can very carefully buy 'flour' tortillas, but be sure the flour is purely maize flour and gluten-free.

Corn and Clam Chowder

If you like your chowder thick and creamy, this is the recipe for you.
If you like it to be very 'brothy' just add more clam juice or cream.

1. Place the clams in a large pot with a cup of water and steam, covered, over high heat. When the clams have opened, cool, remove from the shells and chop in a food processor. Reserve the clam juice.

2. Sauté the bacon in a large pot. Place on paper towels to drain. Add the onion, peppers and thyme to the pot and sauté until softened, about 10 minutes.

3. If the pot is dry, add a tablespoon of butter or oil. Stir in the cornflour and cook for 3 minutes. Add the chopped clams, sweetcorn and extra clam juice.

4. Cover and simmer for 20 minutes. Just before serving, add the cream, salt, pepper, and parsley. Serve in warm bowls with gluten-free scones, hot cornbread or crackers.

Makes 12 cups

18 cherrystone or 12 large
    clams, scrubbed and
    checked to make sure
    they are closed
6 rashers streaky bacon
1 onion, chopped
1 green pepper, cored,
    seeded and chopped
1 red pepper, cored,
    seeded and chopped
2 jalapeño chillies, cored,
    seeded and chopped
    (optional)
1 teaspoon dried thyme
1 tablespoon butter or oil (as
    needed)
2 tablespoons cornflour or
    rice flour
1¼lb frozen sweetcorn, or
    the kernels from 6 ears
    fresh corn
1 pint fish stock
1½ pints single cream
Salt to taste
Freshly ground black pepper
    to taste
Chopped fresh parsley

Corn and Lobster Newburg

*Buy three small cooked lobsters (weighing about 1¼lb each), or
frozen lobster meat. Serve this dish with rice and salad.*

2 tablespoons unsalted butter
2 shallots, chopped
4 egg yolks
2 cups cream
1 cup fresh sweetcorn, cut
    off the cob, or frozen
    sweetcorn, blanched
    and drained
1½lb or 4 cups lobster meat
2 tablespoons dry sherry
2 tablespoons chopped
    parsley for garnish

1. Melt the butter and sauté the shallots for 5–6 minutes until soft. In a small bowl, beat the egg yolks.

2. Put the cream into a large pan over a medium heat; scald the cream but do not boil. Remove from the heat. Mix 2 tablespoons of hot cream into the beaten eggs and whisk vigorously.

3. Pour the egg mixture into the hot cream and return to the heat. Continue to whisk until thick. Add the corn and lobster. Heat, stirring, until very hot but not boiling. Add the sherry. Serve garnished with parsley.

Scalding Cream or Water

Scalding is when you heat a liquid to just short of boiling. When you see tiny bubbles around the edge of the pot, the liquid is technically scalded. Scalding is useful to prevent curdling or overheating. The water in the bottom of a double boiler should, in most cases, be scalding hot, not boiling, or it will overflow and make a mess.

Extra Egg Whites or Yolks

The recipe for Lobster Newburg calls for 4 egg yolks. This gives you the opportunity to make a marvellous meringue for dessert with the whites. Or if you have a recipe that calls for whites and not yolks, you can make mayonnaise or custard with the yolks. There is a use for everything but the shells.

Golden Corn Fritters

Fritters are really fun to make and to eat.
They can be as plain or as interesting as you want. The idea is to make them
really creamy on the inside and golden on the outside.

Makes 12–14 fritters

1 egg
⅓ cup milk or gluten-free beer
⅔ cup cornflour or maize flour (masa harina)
1½ teaspoons gluten-free baking powder
½ teaspoon salt
Red chilli flakes and/or ground black pepper to taste
⅛ teaspoon freshly grated nutmeg
1 cup fresh sweetcorn, cut off the cob, or frozen
Groundnut, canola or other cooking oil (not olive oil)

1. Starting with the egg and milk, place everything but the sweetcorn and oil in a food processor and blend until smooth. Scrape into a bowl; fold in the sweetcorn.

2. Heat about 1in of oil to 180°C/350°F.

3. Drop the fritters by the tablespoonful into the hot oil. Drain on paper towels and serve hot.

Frittering Away

You can vary your fritters by using chopped clams instead of corn. Fritters are fine with eggs for breakfast or as a side dish with chicken or steak. They are good with syrup or savoury with gravy. You can also use them as hors d'oeuvres to dip in salsa.

Corn Fritters Stuffed with Oysters

Makes 12 fritters

1 egg
⅓ cup milk or gluten-free beer
⅔ cup cornflour or maize flour (masa harina)
1½ teaspoons gluten-free baking powder
½ teaspoon salt
Red chilli flakes and/or ground black pepper to taste
⅛ teaspoon freshly grated nutmeg
1 cup fresh sweetcorn, cut off the cob, or frozen
6 large oysters, shucked
Oil for frying

These fritters are delightful – they puff up nicely and become very fluffy, and the oyster morsels add flavour. Serve with a fresh spinach salad.

1. Starting with the egg and milk, place everything but the sweetcorn, oysters and oil in a food processor and blend until smooth. Scrape into a bowl; fold in the sweetcorn.

2. Poach the oysters whole in ½ cup boiling water. When the edges curl, they are done. Cool and chop them, then fold them into the batter. Add extra flour if the batter is too thin.

3. Heat the oil to 180°C/350°F. Drop the fritters by the tablespoonful into the hot oil. Drain on paper towels and serve hot.

Stocking Up

Be sure to look into all the wonderful gluten-free products you can buy in health food stores and on the Web. If you are making crêpes, make an extra-large batch – they are easy to freeze, layered between sheets of greaseproof paper. Then you can take them out and use them as you need them.

Indian Corn Cakes

This is a good side dish served with game such as rabbit or venison.
Juniper berries are popular in North American Indian and all Norse cooking.

∾

1. Bring the water to the boil and add salt. Stir in the cornmeal and cook for about 20 minutes, stirring. Add the pepper, black treacle and juniper berries.

2. Oil an 11 x 13in glass lasagne dish. Spread the corn mixture in the dish and cover. Refrigerate for 1–2 hours or until very stiff.

3. Heat butter or lard in a large frying pan. Cut the corn mixture into square cakes and fry until golden on both sides.

Makes about 12 cakes

7 cups water
1 tablespoon salt, or to taste
2 cups cornmeal
½ teaspoon freshly ground
    black pepper, or to taste
1 teaspoon black treacle
10 juniper berries, crushed
    in a mortar and pestle
    (optional)
4 tablespoons butter or lard

Corn Lore

Native Americans saved early European settlers with their stores of corn. They taught the colonists how to grow, dry and mill corn into meal. Interestingly, corn as a crop started in ancient Mexico and Central America. The valuable crop spread all the way to Canada, indicating tribal movement and sharing.

Maple Corn Cakes

Makes 12 medium-sized pancakes

2 cups rice flour
5 teaspoons baking powder
1 teaspoon salt
2 tablespoons maple syrup
2 cups milk
2 eggs
1 tablespoon butter, melted
1½ cups sweetcorn (fresh or frozen)
Butter or oil for the griddle

This is a wonderful quick supper for the kids, also good for brunch or breakfast. Serve with bacon, sausages or ham and eggs if you are really hungry.

1. Mix the dry ingredients together in a bowl.

2. Slowly add the syrup, milk, eggs and butter, whisking to keep it light. Fold in the sweetcorn.

3. Heat a griddle or large frying pan over a medium heat. Drop the cakes on the buttered griddle using a ladle. Fry until little bubbles form on the tops of the cakes. Turn and fry on the other side until golden brown. Serve with maple syrup, or fresh berries and whipped cream.

Polenta: A Fancy Name for Good Old Cornmeal

You can buy polenta ready-made but it is expensive and less nourishing than the polenta you make yourself. It can be elegant but usually is simply fried or served in a soft, creamy mound, like mashed potatoes. It's good with any sauce or gravy; it's so very bland that you really need to spice it up.

Classic Polenta with Herbs and Parmesan

Use 7 cups of water if you want soft polenta the consistency of mashed pota-toes; use 6½ cups if you prefer it firm enough to cut into squares to grill or fry.

1. Bring the water to the boil.

2. Add salt, and using your hand to drop the cornmeal into the boiling water, let the cornmeal slip slowly between your fingers in a very slim stream. You should be able to see each grain. Don't dump the cornmeal into the water or you will get a mass of glue.

3. Stir constantly while adding the cornmeal. Reduce the heat to a simmer and keep stirring for about 20 minutes as the polenta thickens.

4. Stir in the butter, herbs, Parmesan cheese and pepper. If you're making soft polenta, serve immediately. If you're making firm polenta, spread in an oiled 9 x 13in lasagne dish. Chill for 3 hours or overnight. Cut into sections and fry, grill or barbecue.

The Staple of Lombardy

Polenta has been the staple food of Lombardy, at the foot of the Italian Alps, for three centuries. Thanks to Columbus and his sailors, corn, peppers, and other staples from America have augmented the diet of much of Europe.

Serves 4–6

6½ or 7 cups water
2 tablespoons salt
2 cups yellow cornmeal
2–4oz unsalted butter
2 tablespoons dried herbs
or 1 tablespoon each
chopped fresh basil,
rosemary and parsley
½ cup freshly grated
Parmesan cheese
Freshly ground black pepper
to taste

Polenta with Sun-Dried Tomatoes and Basil

Makes 12 squares

8oz sun-dried tomatoes in oil, chopped finely

20 basil leaves

2 cloves garlic

1 recipe Classic Polenta with Herbs and Parmesan (see page 175), prepared to be firm

Extra olive oil, if necessary

1 cup grated mozzarella cheese

The fascinating thing about polenta is that you can change the seasonings and/or toppings and fry, grill, or barbecue, to get a different dish, based on polenta, time after time.

1. Preheat the oven to 180°C/350°F/Gas 4.

2. Whizz the tomatoes, basil and garlic in a food processor. The mixture should be chunky, not puréed. Add extra olive oil if it is too dry to process. Spread the tomato mixture over the polenta and cut into squares.

3. Place the squares on a buttered baking sheet. Bake for 20 minutes.

4. At the last minute, sprinkle the mozzarella over the top and bake until the cheese has melted. Serve immediately.

Polenta with Chillies and Cheddar Cheese

Serves 6–7

1 recipe Classic Polenta with Herbs and Parmesan (see page 175), prepared to be firm

1 cup salsa (mild, medium or hot, to taste)

4 jalapeño chillies, cored, seeded and chopped

1½ cups coarsely grated mature Cheddar cheese

Sour cream to garnish, 1 tablespoon per square of polenta

This has a spicy flavour. You'll love it with ham, pork or a barbecue. It's also good with split pea soup.

1. When the polenta is firm, cut it in portion-sized squares and place on an oiled baking sheet.

2. Preheat the oven to 180°C/350°F/Gas 4. Mix together the salsa, peppers and cheese. Spoon over the top of the squares of polenta.

3. Bake until the polenta is very hot and the cheese is melted in the sauce. Arrange on plates and spoon a dollop of sour cream over each.

Chapter 13
Salsas and Chutneys

Green Tomato Salsa

*At the end of summer, tart unripe green tomatoes
make a fresh-tasting spicy salsa.*

Makes about 1 cup

10–12 green tomatoes,
    chopped
2 tablespoons olive oil
½ red onion, finely chopped
2 cloves garlic, chopped
Juice of 1 lime and ½
    teaspoon grated lime zest
2 serrano (hot) chillies, cored,
    seeded and chopped
1 teaspoon salt, or to taste
¼ cup chopped parsley or
    coriander

Combine all the ingredients in a bowl and cover. Leave to stand for 2 hours or refrigerate overnight. Serve at room temperature.

Spicy Tomato Salsa

*Salsa made with fresh tomatoes and herbs is such a treat.
Of course, you can vary it tremendously.
Have fun with it, adding extras from your garden.*

Makes about 1½ cups

10 large, fresh plum or Roma
    tomatoes, blanched in
    boiling water, skinned
¼ cup lemon juice
3 cloves garlic, chopped
2 ears cooked fresh
    sweetcorn, kernels cut
    from the cob
1 teaspoon cumin
2 onions, peeled, cut into
    quarters
Salt and hot pepper sauce
    to taste
½ cup chopped fresh
    coriander or parsley,
    to taste

Mix all the ingredients in a food processor, pulsing until coarsely chopped. Refrigerate until ready to serve.

Apple, Cranberry and Walnut Chutney

This is excellent with duckling, chicken and, of course, turkey. It's easy to make and will keep for 2 weeks in the refrigerator. Or make a lot and freeze it.

1. Cook the shallots in the oil in a large, heavy saucepan until softened.

2. Mix everything but the walnuts in with the shallots. Cook, stirring, until the berries have popped and the sauce has become very thick.

3. Cool and stir in the toasted walnut pieces. Store in the refrigerator.

Fruit and Pepper

Try putting some pepper on watermelon, cantaloupe or honeydew melon. You'll find that peppery chutneys and salsas make an excellent accompaniment to all kinds of dishes.

Makes 2 cups

½ cup finely chopped shallots
2 tablespoons cooking oil
2 cups cranberries, fresh or
  frozen
2 tart apples, peeled, cored,
  and chopped
½ cup brown sugar, or to
  taste
¼ cup cider vinegar
2 tablespoons water
1 teaspoon orange zest
½ teaspoon ground coriander
½ teaspoon black pepper
½ teaspoon salt
½ cup walnut pieces, toasted

Mango, Cherry, and Apricot Chutney

Make a double quantity – it's so good, you'll want more.
It's wonderful with swordfish and prawns.

Makes 1½ cups

2 ripe mangos, peeled and
    chopped
½ cup dried cherries, soaked
    in ½ cup hot water
2–3 ripe apricots, blanched,
    peeled, halved and pitted
1 jalapeño chilli, cored,
    seeded and chopped
1 tablespoon chopped fresh
    ginger
1 tablespoon brown sugar, or
    to taste
2 shallots, chopped
Juice of 1 large lemon

Combine all the ingredients in a bowl and mix well. Cover and refrigerate overnight. Serve at room temperature. (This will keep for 2–3 days in the fridge.)

Root Ginger

Although ginger, a true spice, is wonderful in Asian dishes, it's also very good in beef and lamb stews. Grandmothers used to crumble up ginger snaps to add to stews and stuffings. Ginger keeps well in the refrigerator or freezer and all you have to do is break off a chunk, peel it, and chop it. Dried ginger is also available, but fresh is so much better.

Tropical Fruit Salsa

The sweet-hot combination is wonderful.
Try it with pork, lamb or any kind of fish.

Mix all the ingredients in a bowl and cover. Refrigerate for 2 hours. Serve at room temperature.

Chillies – Handle with Care

When handling chillies, it's very wise to wear rubber gloves. If they burn your mouth, they can also burn your skin. If you do not use gloves, be sure to wash your hands immediately and thoroughly after handling chillies. And be careful with them. Anything punishingly hot will kill taste buds, so you will need more and more heat over time to taste it at all.

Makes about 1½ cups

1 large mango, peeled,
     seeded and diced
1 cup fresh pineapple, diced
¼ cup chopped red onion
1 teaspoon Tabasco sauce, or
     to taste
½ teaspoon freshly grated
     lime zest
Juice of ½ lime
Salt to taste

Sweet and Hot Pineapple Salsa

Makes 2 cups

1½ cups fresh pineapple
   chunks
2 tablespoons brown sugar
1 tablespoon hot pepper
   sauce
¼ cup fresh lemon juice
Salt to taste
½ teaspoon ground coriander
½ cup chopped sweet red
   onion

This is delicious any time of year.

Put all the ingredients into a food processor and pulse until coarsely chopped. Vary with chopped, toasted nuts, and/or crisp bits of apple.

Food Processor Sense

Today you can buy small, medium or large food processors. To prevent mess, process your food in batches. Otherwise the liquid will spill out and make a mess of your machine and your worktop.

Green Sauce

Makes 1½ cups

1 recipe Basic Aioli (see
   page 203) or 1½ cups
   commercial mayonnaise
¼ cup snipped fresh dill
½ cup chopped fresh parsley
6 fresh basil leaves, torn
1 teaspoon coarsely ground
   pepper
Extra lemon juice, optional

*This is another versatile sauce, wonderful over
seafood, vegetables or chicken.*

Whizz all the ingredients in a blender or food processor. Store in the refrigerator.

Green Sauce for Salmon

Green sauce is popular with salmon. It can be made with different herbs, mayonnaise and lemon juice. The point is to use lots of fresh green herbs to give it that great colour and flavour.

Mango Salsa

This is quick and easy. Try it with cold chicken, seafood or grilled fish.

Mix all ingredients together and leave to stand for 2 hours or in the fridge overnight. Serve at room temperature or cold.

Makes about 1 cup

2 ripe mangos, peeled, seeded, and chopped
1 jalapeño chilli, or to taste, chopped
Juice of 1 lime
1 teaspoon lime zest
2 tablespoons chopped red onion
1 teaspoon sugar
Salt to taste
¼ cup chopped fresh mint or parsley

Curry-Mustard Mayonnaise

This is fabulous in a rice salad with seafood or chicken. It's excellent with grilled vegetables.

Whisk all the ingredients together in a bowl, cover and refrigerate. Variations include adding herbs, green peppercorns or capers.

Makes 1½ cups

1 recipe Basic Aioli (see page 203) or 1½ cups commercial mayonnaise
2 teaspoons curry powder, or to taste
2 teaspoons Dijon mustard, or to taste
1 tablespoon lemon juice
Dash Tabasco

Curry-Mustard Sauce

A classic use of curry-mustard mayonnaise is in the French recipe for chicken salad Boulestin, with chunks of chicken and rice. It is also good in a rice and vegetable salad. Try it also as a dipping sauce for prawns.

Classic Red Tomato Salsa

Makes 1½–2 cups

*Your own homemade salsa with red,
ripe tomatoes tastes so much better than jarred!*

6 large, ripe, juicy red
   tomatoes
2 cloves garlic
2 serrano or jalapeño chillies,
   or to taste, cored, seeded,
   and chopped
½ cup chopped sweet white
   onion
Juice of 1 lime
1 teaspoon salt, or to taste
½ cup chopped coriander

Put all the ingredients in a food processor and pulse until well blended. Do not purée. Serve after 1 hour or refrigerate overnight. You can vary the amount of chillies to taste.

Salsa Style

Salsa is a Mexican invention, using the hot and sweet chillies, tomatoes, herbs and spices available. Hot food has a purpose in a hot climate: it makes you sweat, and when you sweat, you cool off – a bit. Foods that are extremely hot do kill taste buds, so don't punish your mouth.

Incredible Hollandaise Sauce

This sauce can be varied enormously. It's perfect on fish, lobster or hot vegetables, especially asparagus, artichokes and broccoli.

Makes 1¼ cups

8oz unsalted butter
1 whole egg and 1 or 2 egg
    yolks, depending on the
    richness desired
1 tablespoon freshly
    squeezed lemon juice
⅛ teaspoon cayenne pepper
Salt to taste

1. Melt the butter in a small, heavy saucepan over a very low heat. Put the eggs, lemon juice and cayenne in a blender or food processor. Blend well.

2. With the motor running on low, add the hot butter, a little at a time, to the egg mixture.

3. Return to the pan you used to melt the butter. Whisking, thicken the sauce over a low heat, adding salt. As soon as it is thick, pour into a bowl, a sauce boat or over the food. (Reheating the sauce to thicken it is the delicate stage. You must not let it get too hot or it will scramble the eggs, or even curdle them. If either disaster happens, add a tablespoon of boiling water and whisk like mad.)

Hollandaise Sauce

The name implies that this sauce was created in Holland, a land of high butter use. However, it is not called Holland sauce; we get a French spelling. In any area where there is plentiful butter, hollandaise sauce, with its rich, smooth texture, will reign.

Sauce Maltaise

This is a wonderful variation on hollandaise sauce that is perfect with fish, seafood, chicken or vegetables.

Makes 1 cup

8oz unsalted butter
1 whole egg and 1 or 2 egg yolks, depending on the richness desired
1 tablespoon freshly squeezed orange juice
½ teaspoon grated orange zest
⅛ teaspoon cayenne pepper
Salt to taste
Tabasco sauce to taste (optional)

1. Melt the butter in a small, heavy saucepan over a very low heat. Put the eggs, orange juice, orange zest, salt and cayenne in a blender or food processor. Blend well. Season to taste and add Tabasco if desired.

2. With the motor running on low, add the hot butter, a little at a time, to the egg mixture.

3. Return to the pan you used to melt the butter. Whisking, thicken the sauce over low heat, and as soon as it is thick, pour into a bowl, a sauce boat or over the food. (Reheating the sauce to thicken it is the delicate stage. You must not let it get too hot or it will scramble the eggs, or even curdle them. If either disaster happens, add a tablespoon of boiling water and whisk like mad.) Serve immediately.

Sauce Béarnaise

This classic sauce is usually served with fillet steak, prime rib of beef or fish. It's excellent with swordfish or salmon.

Makes 1¼ cups

8oz unsalted butter
1 whole egg and 1 or 2 egg
*   yolks, depending on the*
*   richness desired*
1 tablespoon white wine
*   vinegar*
½ teaspoon dried tarragon
⅛ teaspoon cayenne pepper
Salt to taste

1. Melt the butter in a small, heavy saucepan over a very low heat. Put the eggs, vinegar, tarragon and cayenne in a blender or food processor. Blend well.

2. With the motor running on low, add the hot butter, a little at a time, to the egg mixture.

3. Return to the pan you used to melt the butter. Add salt. Whisking, thicken the sauce over low heat, and as soon as it is thick, pour into a bowl, a sauce boat or over the food. (Reheating the sauce to thicken it is the delicate stage. You must not let it get too hot or it will scramble the eggs, or even curdle them. If either disaster happens, add a tablespoon of boiling water and whisk like mad.)

Sweet and Tart Whipped Prune and Brandy Sauce

Makes 1 cup

½ cup pitted prunes
½ cup cognac or brandy
¼ teaspoon allspice
½ cup double cream
¼ teaspoon ground black
    pepper

*This is a natural with game. It's also wonderful with turkey and pork.
Just put a tablespoonful over whatever you've cooked and it's great.*

1. Soak the prunes in the brandy until they are plump. Whizz the prune/ brandy mixture with the allspice in the blender and set aside.

2. Whip the cream with the pepper until stiff.

3. Warm the brandy/prune mixture, fold in the whipped cream, and serve.

Brandy as a Spice and Flavouring

Adding brandy to a sauce or stew will give you a wonderful nutty nuance. The alcohol cooks away and evaporates. Don't worry – no one will get tipsy on a brandy sauce. When it's added to a brown gravy or cream sauce, it's sublime.

White and Red Grape Sauce for Poultry and Game

*This is wonderful with chicken, turkey or duck.
For an exciting taste, try it with venison.*

Makes 2 cups

*2 tablespoons unsalted butter
2 shallots, chopped
2 tablespoons cornflour
1 cup chicken stock, warmed
½ cup seedless red grapes,
    washed and halved
½ cup seedless green grapes,
    washed and halved
¼ cup dry white wine
1 teaspoon rosemary
10 fresh basil leaves
1 teaspoon Worcestershire
    sauce
Salt and pepper to taste*

1. Melt the butter and sauté the shallots. When they are soft, after about 5 minutes over medium heat, stir in the cornflour; cook for 4 minutes. Whisk in the warm stock and add the grapes, wine and herbs. (For a variation, you can add half a cup of double cream or some lemon juice.) Bring to the boil and cook for 10 minutes, until the grapes are soft.

2. Add the Worcestershire sauce, salt and pepper. Serve hot.

Chutney

The British fell in love with chutney when they ruled India. You can buy basic chutneys in the supermarket; however, a good Indian cook will make chutney especially to go with what he or she is serving. It's wonderful with any cold meat or hot curry.

Redcurrant and Port Sauce for Pork or Game

½ cup redcurrant jelly
½ cup port
¼ cup water
2 teaspoons cornflour
⅛ teaspoon ground cloves
⅛ teaspoon ground allspice
½ teaspoon salt
Freshly ground pepper
    to taste

A little goes a long way, so it's best to serve this in a sauce boat on the side so people can take as much or as little as they please.

1. Heat the jelly and port in a saucepan. Mix the water and cornflour together and whisk it into the jelly/port mixture. Boil for 5 minutes.

2. Add the rest of the ingredients and serve. (To vary the sauce, you can add 1 tablespoon fresh orange juice, 1 teaspoon lemon juice or ¼ cup double cream.)

Au 'Currant'

Redurrants have a nice tart bite to them, but when dried they taste quite sweet. Redurrant jelly is readily available and is classically served with game birds and venison. It is also an excellent condiment for turkey, as an alternative to cranberry sauce.

Pesto with Mint

This is great with lamb, pork and any vegetables.

❧

Makes about 1 cup

½ cup fresh mint
½ cup fresh flat-leaf parsley
¾ cup extra virgin olive oil,
    more if needed
Juice of ½ fresh lemon
½ teaspoon pepper
½ cup blanched almonds,
    toasted
Salt to taste

Whirl all ingredients in a blender. Taste before adding extra salt.

More Mints Than Can Be Imagined

Take a stroll through a herb farm and you will see myriad varieties of mint. Apart from spearmint and peppermint, there is orange mint, lemon mint, and even chocolate mint. Mint grows like a weed and can take over a garden with little encouragement, so it's better to plant it in a container.

Pesto Sauce

This is a classic sauce. It's great with vegetables and spaghetti squash, fine over rice noodles.

❧

Makes 1½ cups

2 cups fresh basil leaves,
    packed
2–3 cloves fresh garlic
1 cup extra virgin olive oil
½ cup pine nuts, toasted
Salt and pepper to taste

Place all the ingredients in a blender and purée. You may need to add a little more olive oil if it seems too dry. Serve immediately.

Spaghetti Squash, the 'Almost' Pasta

We found that we like spaghetti squash as much as pasta. It adapts to any sauce that you would make for gluten-heavy pasta. Use it freely with Bolognese, Alfredo, carbonara and seafood sauces, and with plain old tomato sauce. As a side dish, it's excellent dressed with butter, Parmesan cheese and fresh herbs.

Sweet and Hot Yellow Tomato Coulis

Make 1½ cups

4 large yellow tomatoes,
    cored and chopped
2 cloves garlic, halved
3 shallots, cut up
½ cup extra virgin olive oil
1 tablespoon orange juice
1 tablespoon finely chopped
    parsley
Salt and pepper to taste

*This is excellent drizzled over prawns, fish or poultry. Its fresh
taste will last if it's kept in the refrigerator or freezer.*

Put all the ingredients in a blender. Purée. Serve cold, or warm the sauce
over a low heat.

Tomatoes

*Yellow tomatoes are much sweeter than red ones. They are great fried, cooked
into sauce or made into a coulis. The only trouble with yellow tomatoes is that
they have a short season. When you see them, whether large or cherry-tomato
size, get them, and start eating them out of hand. Or serve them with some
fresh basil and a drizzle of olive oil.*

Sweet Red Pepper Sauce

Makes 1 cup

½ cup roasted red peppers
    packed in oil
1 clove garlic
2 tablespoons lemon juice
4 fresh basil leaves
½ cup sour cream
Salt and pepper to taste

*This takes only a minute or two to prepare – time well spent.
Spoon over grilled vegetables, soups, pork or chicken.
You can use it as a dip with crisps.*

1. Whizz the roasted peppers, garlic, lemon juice and basil in a blender,
    then pour into a bowl.

2. Whisk in the sour cream, then add salt and pepper. Serve chilled.

Courgette Sauce for Seafood

This is excellent with grilled prawns, scallops or poultry.

৩৩

Put all the ingredients in a blender. Purée. Serve warm or cold.

Making Interesting Sauces and Coulis

When you purée such vegetables as roasted red peppers and cooked summer squash and courgettes, you get a nice, creamy base for flavours. Add your favourite herbs and fresh lemon, lime or orange juice. You can adjust the heat to your personal taste. You can also add cream, sour cream or mayonnaise for extra smoothness.

Makes 1½ cups

1 cup steamed courgettes
2 cloves garlic
¼ cup chicken stock
2 tablespoons chopped
    shallot
2 tablespoons lime juice
¼ cup olive oil
Salt and Tabasco sauce to
    taste

Roasted Garlic Sauce with Cream and Cheese

Roasting garlic changes its flavour. It becomes milder, softer and sweeter.

৩৩

1. Preheat the oven to 150°C/300°F/Gas 2.

2. Wrap the dampened garlic in aluminium foil and roast in the oven for 60 minutes. Cool until you can handle it. Cut off the tips and squeeze the garlic pulp out of the skins; set aside.

3. Melt the butter over a low heat and stir in the cornflour. Continue to cook for a few minutes over a low heat. Whisk in the chicken stock, parsley and olive oil.

4. Add the vinegar or lemon juice, salt, pepper and cheese. Whizz all the ingredients in a blender. Pour into a serving bowl and use with vegetables, spaghetti squash, salads, rice or tomatoes.

Makes ¾ cup

1 head garlic unpeeled,
    dampened
1 tablespoon unsalted butter
1 teaspoon cornflour
¼ cup chicken stock
2 tablespoons chopped
    flat-leaf parsley
2 tablespoons olive oil
1 teaspoon vinegar or lemon
    juice
Salt and pepper to taste
2 tablespoons grated
    Parmesan cheese
½ cup double cream

Caper Sauce for Fish, Meat or Poultry

Makes ½ cup

These Mediterranean ingredients will enhance any number of entrées. You can use this on most dishes as a sauce and/or flavouring.

4 tablespoons unsalted butter
1 tablespoon extra virgin olive oil
2 large shallots, chopped
1 clove garlic, chopped
3 tablespoons capers
¼ cup dry white wine
1 teaspoon lemon juice
½ cup chopped parsley
4 mint leaves, shredded
Salt and pepper to taste

1. Heat the butter, olive oil and shallots in a saucepan and sauté, stirring, for 5 minutes.

2. Add the rest of the ingredients and cook, stirring, for another 5 minutes. Pour over fish, poultry, steak or grilled vegetables.

Shallots

Shallots are both sweet and aromatic. Try roasting them, or caramelizing them in a pan with a bit of butter. They are part of the onion family but a gentle part. They are milder than onions, and some people think they have a garlicky flavour. They are quite versatile.

White Wine Sauce

You can vary the herbs or add some sliced mushrooms, olives, capers or green peppercorns. Pour the sauce over any fish or meat, mashed potatoes or rice.

1. Sauté the onion for 4 minutes in the butter and oil. Whisk in the cornflour and cook for 3–4 minutes.

2. Whisk in the warm chicken stock, stirring until smooth. Then add the wine or vermouth. Swirl in the mustard, herbs, salt and pepper. Simmer over a low heat for 10 minutes, stirring occasionally.

3. Add cream if desired. Serve hot.

Makes 1½ cups

½ cup chopped sweet onion
2 tablespoons unsalted butter
1 tablespoon extra virgin
   olive oil
3 tablespoons cornflour
1 cup chicken stock, warmed
½ cup dry white wine or dry
   vermouth
½ teaspoon prepared Dijon
   mustard
¼ cup chopped parsley
1 teaspoon shredded fresh
   basil
½ teaspoon dried tarragon or
   rosemary
Salt and pepper to taste
½ cup double cream
   (optional)

Red Wine Sauce

*Once you've had this with fillet steak, prime rib of beef
or an elegant hamburger, you'll make it often.*

Makes 2 cups

4 shallots, peeled and
  chopped finely
2 cloves garlic, or to taste,
  chopped
2 tablespoons butter
2 tablespoons olive oil
1 cup sliced mushrooms,
  brown, white button or
  exotic
3 teaspoons potato, maize or
  rice flour
1 cup beef stock, heated
1 cup red wine, such as
  Burgundy or Merlot
1 tablespoon Worcestershire
  sauce
Salt and pepper to taste

1. Sauté the shallots and garlic in butter and oil in a large saucepan over a low heat. Toss the mushrooms to coat in the butter and oil. Blend in the flour and simmer for 10 minutes, stirring.

2. Whisk in the stock and red wine, Worcestershire sauce, salt and pepper. Bring to the boil. Reduce the heat and simmer the sauce over a very low heat for 20 minutes.

Variations on a Theme

There are many, many different variations on this recipe. There is much to love about this very simple and basic sauce – that's why it's been popular for more than 200 years. Try different herbs such as parsley, rosemary or basil. You can add heat using a few drops of hot red pepper sauce such as Tabasco. Capers, chopped olives or green peppercorns also add a nice touch.

Chapter 14

Pasta Dishes and Sauces

Alfredo Sauce with Parsley

*The eggs in Alfredo sauce are generally cooked by the hot pasta
or mixed with the pasta to cook.*

Makes 1½ cups

1 tablespoon unsalted butter
2 tablespoons chopped
    shallots
1 cup double cream
1 cup petit pois, frozen are
    fine (optional)
½ cup grated Parmesan
    cheese
2 large eggs
1 tablespoon cracked
    peppercorns, or to taste
Salt to taste
½ cup chopped fresh parsley

1. Melt the butter and sauté the shallots for 3–4 minutes. Add the double cream. If using the peas, cook in the hot cream. Bring to the boil, and thicken, cooking for about 6 minutes, stirring constantly.

2. Remove from the heat and stir in the cheese. In a separate, large serving bowl, beat the eggs. Whisk in a tablespoon of the cream sauce; stirring constantly, add the remainder of the sauce, a little at a time. (Be careful – if you put the hot sauce into the eggs too quickly, they will scramble.)

3. Add pepper, salt and parsley. Pour the sauce over spaghetti squash or rice noodles.

Cracked Peppercorns

When a recipe calls for cracked or coarsely ground black pepper, there's an easy way to prepare it. Place a tablespoon or so of peppercorns on a chopping board. Press a heavy frying pan down on the peppercorns and rock it around gently. You will then have cracked pepper. Many pepper grinders also have a setting for coarse grind. You generally have to loosen the screw at the top of the grinder to make the pepper coarse.

Carbonara Sauce

This is not for someone on a diet; however, it's very delicious and easy to make.

Makes 1½ cups

1. Cook the bacon over a low heat until it is fried crisp, then remove it to paper towels and crumble. Reserve the fat. Sauté the shallots in the bacon fat. Add the black pepper and cream. Bring to the boil and cook over a medium-low heat until thick.

2. Mix the eggs and cheese in a bowl. Add a tablespoon of the sauce, whisking. Continue to add sauce slowly, whisking constantly. Add the parsley, crumbled rosemary, reserved bacon and pepper.

3. Pour over rice noodles or spaghetti squash. (You probably won't need salt because there's salt in the bacon.)

4 rashers streaky bacon
4 shallots, chopped
2 teaspoons coarsely ground
    black pepper
1 cup double cream
2 eggs, beaten
½ cup grated Parmesan
    cheese
¼ cup chopped fresh parsley
1 tablespoon fresh rosemary,
    or 1 teaspoon dried,
    crumbled
1 teaspoon cracked black
    peppercorns, or to taste

Carbonara Fan

The origins of carbonara are found in Italy, but whether it comes from Rome or the Lazio region is uncertain. Food writer Calvin Trillin, author of The Tummy Trilogy, *is such a fan of carbonara sauce that he suggested it should replace turkey as the American holiday dish on Thanksgiving Day.*

Basic White Sauce

This cream sauce is the basis for a lot of cooking.
You can use milk instead of cream, but don't substitute margarine for butter.

Makes 2 cups

3 tablespoons unsalted butter
3 tablespoons maize flour
    (masa harina)
2 cups milk or cream, warmed
Salt and pepper to taste

optional:
    ⅛ teaspoon nutmeg, 1
    teaspoon Dijon mustard,
    or 1 tablespoon snipped
    fresh chives

1. Melt the butter and stir in the flour. Sauté, stirring, for 4–5 minutes over a medium-low heat. Add the warm milk or cream, whisking constantly until thickened to the desired consistency.

2. Just before serving, add salt and pepper. Optional ingredients can be added at this time.

Beyond the Basics

Once you learn to make a basic white sauce, you can add mustard, sautéed mushrooms, oysters, prawns, herbs and all kinds of luscious things. Pour the sauce over fish or shellfish, poultry and/or vegetables.

Creamy Cheddar Sauce with Ham and Sherry

*This variation on a basic white sauce is excellent on
vegetables, spaghetti squash or rice.*

1. Melt the butter and stir in the flour. Sauté, stirring, for 4–5 minutes over a medium-low heat. Add the warm milk or cream, whisking constantly until thickened to the desired consistency.

2. Remove from the heat and stir in the cheese, ham, sherry, salt and pepper. Serve.

Sherry as a Flavouring

There are several kinds of sherry used in cooking, dry and sweet. Sweet sherry is often called cream sherry, as in Harveys Bristol Cream. Really good sherry is made in Spain and exported all over the world. The Chinese love it in sauces and soups, and it does add a wonderful flavour. It's also good in prawn bisque, lobster Newburg and other seafood dishes.

Makes 2½ cups

3 tablespoons unsalted butter
3 tablespoons maize flour
    (masa harina)
2 cups milk or cream, warmed
⅔ cup grated mature
    Cheddar cheese
¼ cup chopped smoked ham
2 teaspoons sherry
Salt and pepper to taste

Rich Cream Sauce with
Prosciutto, Gorgonzola, and Walnuts

Makes 2½ cups

3 tablespoons unsalted butter
3 tablespoons maize flour
(masa harina)
2 cups whipping cream,
warmed
2 tablespoons chopped
prosciutto ham
½ cup crumbled Gorgonzola
or blue cheese
¼ teaspoon ground nutmeg
½ cup walnut pieces, toasted
Salt and pepper to taste

This is another delicious variation on the basic white sauce.

1. Melt the butter and stir in the flour. Sauté, stirring for 4–5 minutes over a medium-low heat. Add the warm cream, whisking constantly until thickened to the desired consistency.

2. Remove from the heat and stir in the prosciutto, cheese, nutmeg, walnuts, salt and pepper. Serve immediately.

Rich Cream Sauces Are Versatile

You can add herbs, stock, or even bacon to a rich cream sauce. You can add cheese such as mascarpone or some prosciutto ham! The addition of mushrooms adds body and flavour too! You can adapt a cream sauce to loads of fish, meat and vegetable dishes and benefit from the lush flavours.

Basic Aioli (French or Italian Mayonnaise)

This is so much tastier than commercial mayonnaise from a jar.
Use room-temperature eggs or the aioli will be too thin.

1. Place the eggs, garlic, mustard, and lemon juice or vinegar in the goblet of an electric blender. Blend vigorously.

2. Turn the motor to low and very slowly add the oils, salt and pepper. Refrigerate in a closed container. (Some variations you can try include adding ½ teaspoon anchovy paste, or to taste; lemon zest; various herbs; ground coriander or anise; chilli sauce; or chopped fresh fennel.)

The Mother of Mayonnaise

Aioli and mayonnaise are made with basically the same ingredients, with one exception: aioli has a lot of garlic in it. It is loaded with character and can be spooned into Mediterranean seafood stews and soups or spread on gluten-free bread and sprinkled with cheese to make tasty croutons.

Makes 1½ cups

2 eggs at room temperature
2 cloves garlic
1 teaspoon gluten-free
    English mustard
1 tablespoon fresh lemon
    juice or white wine
    vinegar
½ cup olive oil
½ cup canola oil
Salt and pepper to taste

Creamy Mushroom and Cognac Sauce

½ cup cognac
4oz dried porcini
3 tablespoons unsalted butter
3 tablespoons chestnut flour
4 shallots, chopped
10oz button mushrooms,
    stems trimmed
¼ teaspoon nutmeg
1 cup beef stock
1 cup double cream
1 tablespoon fresh thyme
Salt and freshly ground black
    pepper to taste

*This is great on gluten-free pasta, polenta, or rice.
Add an extra 1½ cups of stock to the recipe to turn it into soup.*

1. Place the cognac and dried mushrooms in a saucepan and add water to cover. Simmer over a low heat for 10 minutes. Remove from the heat and cool. Purée in a blender until very smooth.

2. Melt the butter and stir in the chestnut flour, stirring until well blended. Add the shallots and button mushrooms, stirring constantly. Whisk in the rest of the ingredients, including the puréed mushroom and cognac mixture. (At this point you can add 1½ cups extra stock to make soup.)

A Simple Staple

Polenta is a staple in Italy and it's hard to ruin it. You can use polenta wherever you'd use pasta, serving it with tomato, vegetable, or cream sauces, or with brown gravy with mushrooms. You can make it soft, to mound on a plate or platter, or firm, frying it in squares.

Ham, Broccoli and Prawn Pasta Sauce

This is excellent on rice noodles.
You can substitute chicken strips for the prawns.

Serves 4

1 head broccoli, stems
removed, divided into
small florets
2 tablespoons olive oil
1 teaspoon sesame seed oil
2 cloves garlic, thinly sliced
4oz smoked ham, finely
chopped
Juice of ½ lemon
½ cup dry white wine
2 tablespoons soy sauce or
Worcestershire sauce
1lb raw prawns, peeled and
deveined
1 teaspoon sugar
½ cup toasted pine nuts and
¼ cup chopped coriander
or parsley to garnish

1. Bring a pot of salted water to the boil. Drop the broccoli into the boiling water and cook for 10 minutes. Drain and set aside.

2. Heat the oils and add the garlic; do not brown. Stir in the ham.

3. Add the broccoli and the rest of the ingredients, except for the pine nuts and coriander. The dish is done when the prawns turn pink. Garnish with pine nuts and chopped coriander or parsley and serve.

Spicy Spinach and Lobster Sauce

Quinoa pasta is high in protein and can be used as you would almost any pasta. Rice pasta is found in Asian stores and some supermarkets.

1. Plunge the lobster into plenty of boiling salted water. Cook for 15 minutes. Cool; crack the shell and remove the meat. Set the meat aside.

2. Melt the butter and add the cornflour, stirring until smooth. Whisk in the chicken stock. Add the cream and heat.

3. Stir in the spinach and cook until wilted. Add the sherry, nutmeg, red chilli flakes, and reserved lobster. Sprinkle with salt and pepper. Serve on quinoa or rice pasta.

Serves 4

1 1½lb lobster
2 tablespoons butter
2 tablespoons cornflour
1 cup hot chicken or fish stock
1 cup double cream
3 cups fresh baby spinach, stems trimmed
1 tablespoon dry sherry
Pinch ground nutmeg
1 teaspoon hot red chilli flakes or cayenne pepper
Salt and pepper to taste

Greek Aubergine and Olive Sauce

Here you have many of the flavours of Greece without the travel. Touches of garlic and mint do not overwhelm. This is great on pasta or rice.

1. Dredge the aubergine cubes in flour and salt. In a saucepan, heat the olive oil over a medium-high heat. Sauté the aubergine until brown.

2. When brown, lower the heat and add the garlic; sauté for another 3 minutes.

3. Add the rest of the ingredients and serve.

Serves 4

1 medium aubergine, peeled and cubed
½ cup rice flour mixed with 1 teaspoon salt
⅓ cup olive oil
2 cloves garlic, chopped
½ cup kalamata or other black Greek olives, pitted and chopped
10 mint leaves, coarsely chopped
½ cup finely snipped chives
Juice of ½ lemon
Extra olive oil if sauce seems dry

Confetti and Rice Pasta with Chicken

This is fun to eat and pretty to look at. The 'confetti' is chopped vegetables. Lots of Parmesan cheese completes the dish.

Serves 4

½ cup olive oil
½ cup finely chopped red pepper
½ cup finely chopped yellow courgette
1 bunch spring onions, finely chopped
2 cloves garlic, finely chopped
½ cup rice or maize flour (masa harina)
1 teaspoon salt
½ teaspoon pepper, or to taste
½ teaspoon dried thyme
¾lb boneless, skinless chicken breast, cut into bite-sized pieces
½ cup chicken stock
8 ripe plum tomatoes, chopped, or 1½ cups canned tomatoes
1 teaspoon dried oregano
1 teaspoon dried basil
1 tablespoon red chilli flakes, or to taste
1lb rice pasta, cooked
1 cup freshly grated Parmesan cheese

1. Heat the olive oil and add the pepper, courgette, spring onions and garlic. Sauté over a medium heat, stirring frequently. While the vegetables are sautéing, mix the flour, salt, pepper and thyme on a piece of grease-proof paper.

2. Dredge the chicken in the flour mixture and sauté along with the vegetables. Add the stock, tomatoes, oregano, basil and plenty of red chilli flakes. Cook, uncovered, for 10 minutes to make sure the chicken is done.

3. Add the rice pasta to the sauce and mix. Sprinkle with plenty of grated Parmesan cheese and serve.

Rice Pasta

Rice pasta is available online and from Asian stores. Many supermarkets also carry it. Soba – Japanese noodles – have both buckwheat flour and wheat flour in them and sometimes the contents are listed in Japanese characters only.

Hazelnut, Sour Cream and Ham Sauce

This is so rich, you don't need much.
It's a very good side dish with seafood, fish or chicken.

Serves 4 as a side dish

½ lb gluten-free pasta
1 cup hazelnuts, toasted and
   peeled
4 shallots, chopped
¼ cup olive oil
1 cup finely diced ham
1½ cups sour cream (not
   low-fat)
Freshly ground black pepper
   and celery salt

1. Cook the pasta according to the package directions. Chop the nuts coarsely in a food processor.

2. While the pasta is cooking, sauté the shallots in olive oil. When soft, about 5 minutes, add the toasted hazelnuts, ham and sour cream.

3. Turn the heat down to low, and as soon as the sour cream is hot, sprinkle the sauce with pepper and celery salt and serve with the pasta.

Hazelnuts

Hazelnuts toast up nicely for use in salads, or you can grind them or chop them to make a crust for a piece of fish or a boneless duck breast.

Chapter 15
Cakes, Cookies, and Cobblers

Baked Ricotta Torte with
Candied Orange Peel and Chocolate Chips

Serves 6–8

5 eggs
1lb ricotta cheese
4oz cream cheese (not low- or nonfat)
1 teaspoon vanilla extract
1 teaspoon salt
¾ cup candied orange peel, chopped
1 cup dark chocolate chips

This is an adaptation of an Italian Christmas torte;
it's rich and a very good easy-to-make finale for a big family dinner.

1. Preheat the oven to 180°C/350°F/Gas 4. Separate the eggs and beat the whites until stiff. Set aside. Put the yolks, cheeses, vanilla and salt in the food processor and whizz until smooth.

2. Place in a bowl and fold in the egg whites, the orange peel, and the chocolate. Grease a pie dish (preferably glass). Pour in the mixture and bake for 45 minutes or until the cake is set and golden on top.

Ricotta Cheese and Curd Cheese

You can substitute curd cheese for ricotta in any recipe. Curd cheese may be a bit moister than ricotta – you can drain it in a sieve lined with muslin.

Chocolate Mint Swirl Cheesecake with Chocolate Nut Crust

This is incredibly rich and delicious. It is definitely a special occasion cake with layers of deep flavour. Serve in small slices, as it's very, very rich.

Serves 10–12

1½ cups ground walnuts (the food processor works well)
½ cup sugar
⅓ cup unsalted butter, melted
8oz dark chocolate
4 eggs, separated
3 8oz packs cream cheese (not low- or nonfat)
1 cup sour cream
¾ cup sugar
1½ teaspoons pure vanilla extract
1 teaspoon salt
2 tablespoons chestnut flour
2 tablespoons peppermint schnapps
Whipped cream for topping (optional)

1. Mix the first three ingredients together and add half the chocolate, melted. Grease a 9in springform cake tin and press the walnut mixture into the bottom to make a crust. Chill for at least 1 hour.

2. Preheat the oven to 180°C/350°F/Gas 4. In a clean bowl, beat the egg whites until stiff. In a separate large bowl, using an electric mixer, beat the cream cheese, sour cream, sugar, vanilla, chestnut flour and salt. Melt the remaining chocolate with the schnapps.

3. With the motor running, add the egg yolks, one at a time, beating vigorously. Fold in the stiff egg whites. Using a knife, swirl the mint chocolate into the bowl.

4. Pour into the cake tin and bake for 1 hour. Turn off the oven, and with the door ajar, let the cake cool for another hour. Chill before serving. You can top with whipped cream before serving.

Baking with Cream Cheese

It's best to use cream cheese that is not low- or nonfat. The lower the fat content, the more chemicals there are in the cheese to make it work for spreading. When baking, use the purest ingredients, as heat will change the consistency of anything artificial.

Cherry Vanilla Cheesecake with Walnut Crust

Serves 10–12

1½ cups ground walnuts
½ cup sugar
½ cup unsalted butter, melted
4 eggs, separated
3 8oz packs cream cheese
1 cup sour cream
2 teaspoons pure vanilla
   extract
1 teaspoon salt
2 tablespoons rice flour
⅔ cup cherry preserve,
   melted

This is a fine combination with a delightful flavour and smooth consistency.

1. Mix together the walnuts, sugar and melted butter. Grease a springform cake tin and press the nut mixture into the bottom to form a crust. Chill for at least 1 hour.

2. Preheat the oven to 180°C/350°F/Gas 4. Beat the egg whites and set aside. In a large bowl, using an electric mixer, beat the cream cheese, sour cream, vanilla, salt and rice flour together.

3. Add the egg yolks, one at a time, while beating. When smooth, fold in the egg whites and mix in the cherry preserve.

4. Pour into the tin and bake for 1 hour. Turn off the oven and leave the door ajar. Leave the cake to cool for another hour. Chill before serving.

Nut Crusts for Cheesecake

We specify walnuts because they work well in these recipes. However, you can substitute hazelnuts, almonds or pecans. Grinding nuts is simple – just use your food processor.

Lemon Cheesecake with Nut Crust

This cheesecake is light, with an intense lemon flavour.
It's a good summer cheesecake that will make your guests ask for more.

Serves 10–12

1¼ cups ground walnuts (or
whatever nuts you like)
½ cup sugar
½ cup unsalted butter, melted
5 egg whites
3 8oz packs cream cheese
1 cup sour cream
⅔ cup sugar
2 tablespoons rice flour
3 egg yolks
Juice of one lemon
Grated rind of 1 lemon
1 teaspoon salt
Extra nuts to sprinkle on
top of cake, paper-thin
lemon slices

1. Mix together the ground nuts, sugar, and melted butter. Grease a springform cake tin. Press the nut mixture into the bottom to form a crust, and chill.

2. Preheat the oven to 180°C/350°F/Gas 4. Beat the egg whites until stiff and set aside. Using an electric mixer, beat the cheese, sour cream, sugar, flour, salt and egg yolks, adding the yolks one at a time. Beat in the lemon juice and lemon rind.

3. Gently fold in the egg whites. Pour the cheese/lemon mixture into the cake tin. Bake for 1 hour. Turn off the oven and leave the cake to cool for another hour with the door ajar. Chill before serving. The chopped nuts and thinly sliced lemon make a nice touch.

Stiffly Beaten Egg Whites

Be very careful not to get even a speck of egg yolk in the whites to be beaten stiff. Even a drop of egg yolk will prevent the whites from stiffening. And always use clean beaters. Any fat or oil will prevent the whites from fluffing up. You can use a drop of vinegar or lemon juice to help them stiffen up.

Molten Lava Dark Chocolate Cake

For such an easy recipe, this looks elegant, and tastes more complex than it is to make. The chestnut flour gives a wonderful underlying flavour.

Serves 8

8 teaspoons butter to grease ramekins
8 tablespoons sugar to coat buttered ramekins
8oz dark chocolate
6oz unsalted butter
3 eggs
3 egg yolks
⅓ cup sugar
1 tablespoon chestnut flour
1 teaspoon vanilla
Raspberry sorbet to serve

1. Butter eight 6oz ramekins and coat with sugar. Preheat the oven to 220°C/425°F/Gas 7. Over a very low heat, melt the chocolate and butter in a heavy saucepan.

2. Beat the eggs, egg yolks, sugar, flour and vanilla for about 10 minutes. Add the chocolate mixture by the tablespoonful at first, to slacken the mixture, then fold in the rest.

3. Divide the mixture between the ramekins. Place them on a baking sheet and bake for 12–13 minutes. The sides should be puffed and the centres very soft. Serve hot with raspberry sorbet spooned into the 'craters'.

Raspberry Coulis

You can use any berry. Heavily seeded berries can be strained though a fine sieve or muslin. Various liqueurs also make nice additions.

Makes 1½ cups

1 pint raspberries
½ cup sugar
¼ cup water, orange juice or fruit liqueur such as peach or cherry

Place the berries in a saucepan with the sugar and water, juice or liqueur. Bring to the boil. Cool and strain.

Strawberry-Blueberry Coulis

This is wonderful on crêpes, ice cream and pancakes. You can also mix it into Rice Pudding (see page 236) for a different take on an old-fashioned dessert.

Place all the ingredients in a saucepan and bring to the boil. Remove from the heat and cool. Whisk until smooth. Serve warm or cool.

Makes 1½ cups

½ pint blueberries
½ pint strawberries
¼ cup water
¼ cup sugar
Small strip orange rind

Molten Sweet White Chocolate Cake

This is delicious with fresh berries and whipped cream spooned into the 'craters'.

1. Butter eight 6oz ramekins and coat with sugar. Preheat the oven to 220°C/425°F/Gas 7. Melt the chocolate and butter over a low heat in a heavy saucepan. In a large bowl, using an electric mixer, beat together the eggs, egg yolks, sugar and flour. Add vanilla and salt.

2. Keep beating and slowly add, by the tablespoonful, a quarter of the white chocolate mixture. When well blended, add the rest of the chocolate mixture, very slowly.

3. Divide between the ramekins, place on a baking sheet, and bake for about 12 minutes. Serve with mixed berries in the 'craters'. You can vary this by using shaved bitter chocolate in the craters, or spoon in ice cream or sorbet.

Serves 8

8 teaspoons butter to grease ramekins
8 tablespoons sugar to coat buttered ramekins
8oz white chocolate
6oz unsalted butter
3 eggs
3 egg yolks
⅓ cup sugar
1 tablespoon chestnut flour
1 teaspoon vanilla
½ teaspoon salt
2 cups mixed berries, such as strawberries, raspberries and blueberries

Orange Carrot Cake

4 eggs, separated
½ cup brown sugar
1½ cups grated carrots
1 tablespoon lemon juice
Grated rind of ½ fresh orange
½ cup maize flour (masa
    harina)
1in fresh ginger, peeled and
    chopped
1½ teaspoons bicarbonate
    of soda
½ teaspoon salt

This delicious cake has a nice zing with the addition of a little lemon juice and the grated orange rind. The ginger adds an appealing sophistication.

1. Liberally butter a springform cake tin and preheat the oven to 160°C/325°F/Gas 3. Beat the egg whites until stiff and set aside.

2. Beat the egg yolks, sugar and carrots together. Add the lemon juice, orange rind and maize flour. When smooth, add the ginger, bicarbonate of soda, and salt. Gently fold in the egg whites.

3. Pour the batter into the prepared cake tin and bake for 1 hour. Test by plunging a skewer into the centre of the cake – if it comes out clean, the cake is done.

What's Up, Doc?

Carrot cake was created during World War II when flour and sugar were rationed. The sweetness of carrots contributed to this cake, and when oranges were available, it became a feast. Cooks used their fuel carefully too, baking and making stews and soups in the oven all at the same time. Sometimes, hard times make for sweet endings.

Classic Pavlova Cake

This light, beautiful, delicate and delicious cake is enhanced by sweet bananas and strawberries.

1. Preheat the oven to 110°C/210°F/Gas ¼.

2. Whisk the egg whites, and as they stiffen, add the vinegar and slowly add the sugar. Spoon on to a baking sheet covered with baking parchment and spread into a circle. Make a depression in the centre.

3. Bake the meringue for 2 hours. Then, turn off the oven and leave the door ajar. Let the meringue rest for another hour. It should become very crisp and lightly browned. Do not store it if the weather is humid.

4. Whip the cream and mix in the caster sugar and vanilla. Slice a layer of bananas over the centre of the cooled meringue. Add a layer of whipped cream. Sprinkle with halved strawberries.

5. Add another layer of whipped cream and decorate with the whole strawberries. Serve immediately or it will get soggy.

Origins of the Pavlova

There is some discussion as to who invented this cake. It was designed to honor the famed ballerina Anna Pavlova, whose admirers came from around the world. Some say it was created in Australia; others say the cake was born in the United States.

Serves 6

4 egg whites
1 teaspoon vinegar
4oz sugar
1 cup double cream
3 tablespoons caster sugar
½ teaspoon vanilla
1 banana, sliced
1lb strawberries, hulled and
  halved, 8 left whole for
  decoration

Pavlova with Chocolate and Bananas

The uses of meringue are myriad—we are giving you just a few.

Serves 6

4 egg whites
1 teaspoon vinegar
4oz sugar

For the filling:
3oz dark chocolate
½ cup unsalted butter
⅓ cup sugar
2 bananas, put in the freezer
    for 20 minutes to firm
1 cup double cream, whipped
    with 2 teaspoons caster
    sugar

1. Preheat the oven to 110°C/210°F/Gas ¼.

2. Whisk the egg whites, and as they stiffen, add the vinegar and slowly add the sugar. Spoon on to a baking sheet covered with baking parchment and spread into a circle. Make a depression in the centre.

3. Bake the meringue for 2 hours. Then, turn off the oven and leave the door ajar. Let the meringue rest for another hour. It should become very crisp and lightly browned. Do not store it if the weather is humid.

4. Melt the chocolate, butter and sugar. Cool until it's still liquid but at room temperature.

5. Peel and slice one banana into the meringue. Spoon half of the chocolate sauce over it. Add the other banana and the remaining sauce, and top with whipped cream.

Blanching

When you blanch a peach, a tomato or a nectarine, you plunge it into boiling water for a minute. You don't cook it, you just loosen the skin. If you are blanching a great many pieces, have a colander next to your pot of boiling water and a pot of iced water in the sink. Use a slotted spoon to remove the fruit from the boiling water, put it into the colander, and then plunge it into the iced water. When it is cool enough to handle, slip off the skin.

Pavlova with Peach Melba Cream

If you love peach melba, you'll absolutely flip over this dessert.
With the crisp meringue, it's just as good as it gets.

1. Preheat the oven to 110°C/210°F/Gas ¼.

2. Whisk the egg whites, and as they stiffen, add the vinegar and slowly add the sugar. Spoon on to a baking sheet covered with baking parchment and spread into a circle.

3. Bake the meringue for 2 hours. Then, turn off the oven and leave the door ajar. Let the meringue rest for another hour. It should become very crisp and lightly browned. Do not store it if the weather is humid.

4. Bring a saucepan of water to the boil. Add the peaches, and when the skin is loosened, remove the peaches and cool. Slip off the peach skin. Stone the peaches and chop the flesh.

5. Place water and gelatine in a blender and leave to stand for 5 minutes so the gelatine can 'bloom'. Add the peaches to the gelatine and water. Blend, and then leave to cool to room temperature.

6. Just before serving, fold the beaten egg whites into the peach mixture. Fold in the whipped cream. Fill the meringue shell with the peach mixture and sprinkle with raspberries.

Serves 6

4 egg whites
1 teaspoon vinegar
4oz sugar

For the filling:
4 peaches
4oz water
1 ¼oz sachet gelatine
3 egg whites, stiffly beaten
1 cup double cream, whipped
4oz fresh raspberries

Meringue Nests with Icy Sorbet and Fruit Filling

Serves 4

6 egg whites
1 teaspoon vinegar
5oz sugar
½ cup walnut pieces,
    coarsely chopped
4 scoops raspberry or
    strawberry sorbet
4 teaspoons chocolate chips
    or shaved dark chocolate
1 cup double cream, whipped
    with 2 tablespoons caster
    sugar

*Follow your taste preferences when filling these meringues –
try different flavours of sorbet and fruit.*

1. Beat the egg whites, slowly adding the vinegar and sugar. Fold in the nuts. Preheat the oven to 250°F.

2. Spoon the meringue in small circles on to a baking sheet covered with baking parchment and use a spoon to make a depression in the centre of each.

3. Bake for 1 hour. Then turn off the oven and leave the door ajar to make sure the meringues are cooked through and crisp.

4. Fill the meringues with fruit sorbet or ice cream. Top with chocolate chips or shaved chocolate and whipped cream.

Meringues Are Perfect for Gluten-Free Desserts

You can flavour meringue with chocolate, vanilla or fruit liqueurs, and meringue nests can be filled with anything you like, from fruit to ice cream.

Chestnut Cookies

These are festive and delicious. Make a lot for a party or to give to friends.

ༀ

1. Chop the chestnuts in a food processor and place in the bowl of an electric mixer. With the motor on low, add the chestnut flour, milk, egg yolks, vanilla, salt, baking powder, sugar and melted butter.

2. Preheat the oven to 180°C/350°F/Gas 4. Fold the egg whites into the chestnut mixture. Drop the mixture by the teaspoonful on to baking sheets lined with baking parchment.

3. Bake for 12–15 minutes. Cool on a rack, and store in an airtight tin.

Chestnuts

Preparing fresh chestnuts can be a real pain! You have to make cross slits in each, then either boil or roast them, and get the shells off. Then you have to peel off the inner skins. This process is time-consuming. However, you can buy canned or vacuum-packed prepared chestnuts and avoid all that work. Of course, your house won't smell of roasted chestnuts, but you'll have more time to enjoy them.

Make about 48 cookies

2oz prepared chestnuts
1½ cups chestnut flour
½ cup milk
2 egg yolks
1 teaspoon vanilla
1 teaspoon salt
2 teaspoons baking powder
½ cup granulated sugar
½ cup unsalted butter, melted
3 egg whites, stiffly beaten

Chocolate Meringue and Nut Cookies

These are crisp and delicious. The nuts add a wonderful crunch.
Use either blanched almonds or hazelnuts.

Makes about 40 cookies

½ cup sugar
¼ cup cocoa powder
⅛ teaspoon salt
3 egg whites (from extra
    large eggs)
⅛ teaspoon cream of tartar
½ cup hazelnuts, lightly
    toasted, skinned, and
    coarsely chopped

1. Preheat the oven to 140°C/275°F/Gas 1. Line two baking sheets with baking parchment. Sift half the sugar with the cocoa into a bowl. Add the salt.

2. Beat the egg whites with the cream of tartar. When peaks begin to form, add the remaining sugar, a teaspoon at a time. Slowly beat in the cocoa mixture. The meringue should be stiff and shiny.

3. Add the chopped nuts. Drop by teaspoonfuls on to the baking parchment. Bake for 45–50 minutes. Cool on a rack. You can store these in an airtight tin or serve them the same day.

Ugly, but Good!

These cookies are known in Italy as 'ugly but good'! Other, kinder descriptions include 'kisses' and 'crisps'. They are a bit lumpy looking, but just try one. This recipe is a simplification of the original, far more time-consuming one.

Apple Cobbler with Cheddar Scone Crust

*This cobbler is very easy to make in advance –
but bake it just an hour before serving.*

1. Preheat the oven to 160°C/325°F/Gas 3. In a large bowl, mix the flour, salt, baking powder and pepper. Cut in the margarine with a large fork until the mixture looks like oatmeal. Add the buttermilk and stir. Add the cheese and set aside.

2. Place the apples in a large baking dish, about 9 x 13in, or a 4-pint casserole. Sprinkle them with lemon juice.

3. Mix together the spices, cornflour, sugars and salt. Toss the apples with this mixture. Dot with butter. Drop the cheese mixture by the tablespoonful over the top.

4. Bake for 50 minutes, or until the crust is browned and the apples are bubbling. Serve with extra slices of cheese or with vanilla ice cream.

Serves 8–10

2 cups maize flour (masa harina)
½ teaspoon salt
4 teaspoons baking powder
½ teaspoon cayenne pepper
¼ cup margarine, softened
¾ cup buttermilk
¾ cup grated mature Cheddar cheese
8 large tart apples such as Granny Smiths, peeled, cored, and sliced
⅓ cup lemon juice
2 teaspoons cinnamon
¼ teaspoon nutmeg
1½ tablespoons cornflour
¼ cup dark brown sugar
¼ cup white sugar
Pinch salt
4 tablespoons butter

Blueberry-Peach Cobbler

6 ripe peaches, blanched in
    boiling water, skinned,
    stoned and sliced
½ cup fresh lemon juice
1 cup sugar
1 pint blueberries, stems
    removed
4oz unsalted butter, melted
½ teaspoon salt
1½ cups rice flour or quinoa
    flour
1 tablespoon baking powder
1 cup buttermilk

*This smells and tastes like August, but if you blanch and freeze your peaches
and buy frozen blueberries, you can reminisce over a past August in January.*

1. Preheat the oven to 190°C/375°F/Gas 5. Slice the peaches into a bowl and sprinkle with lemon juice and half the sugar. Add the blueberries.

2. Butter a 9 x 13in baking dish. Spread the peaches and blueberries over the bottom. Pour the melted butter into a large bowl. Add the remaining sugar and salt and whisk in the flour and baking powder. Add the buttermilk and stir; don't worry about lumps.

3. Drop the batter by tablespoonfuls over the fruit. Bake for 35–40 minutes. Cool for 25 minutes. Serve with vanilla ice cream or whipped cream.

Orange Cornmeal Cookies

3 eggs
1 cup sugar
1½ cups cornmeal
1¼ cup maize flour (masa
    harina)
½ teaspoon salt
¾ teaspoon xanthan gum
6oz unsalted butter, melted
1 tablespoon concentrated
    orange juice
Finely grated zest of ½ orange

*This is an adaptation of a classic Italian cookie. You will love them for the kids
and you can add currants, raisins or dried apple chips.*

1. Whizz the eggs and sugar in a food processor. Slowly add the rest of the ingredients, stopping occasionally to scrape the bowl.

2. Don't overprocess. When the dough comes together, remove from the food processor and wrap in cling film. Refrigerate for 1–2 hours.

3. Preheat the oven to 180°C/350°F/Gas 4. Cover a baking sheet with baking parchment.

4. Break off a small piece of dough and roll into a ball. Flatten and place on the baking sheet. Repeat with the rest of the dough. Bake for 10 minutes, or until golden.

Chapter 16
Puddings, Mousses, and Soufflés

Apple Brown Betty with Cornbread

*In the early days of the United States, no food went to waste.
Thus, stale bread was made into this delicious, homely baked pudding.*

Serves 4

4 large tart apples, peeled,
    cored and sliced
Juice of ½ lemon
2 cups cornbread cubes
2 eggs, lightly beaten
1½ cups milk
1 teaspoon vanilla extract
¼ teaspoon ground nutmeg
1 teaspoon ground cinnamon
⅛ teaspoon ground cloves
½ teaspoon salt
½ cup dark brown sugar, or
    to taste
½ cup butter

1. Preheat the oven to 180°C/350°F/Gas 4. Liberally butter a 4-pint pie dish.

2. Put the apples in the dish and sprinkle with lemon juice. Add the bread cubes. Mix well.

3. Beat together the eggs, milk, vanilla, spices, salt and sugar. Mix with the apples and bread cubes. Dot with butter.

4. Bake for 45 minutes, or until brown on top and very moist inside. Serve warm with whipped cream or ice cream.

Why Use Canned Whipped Cream?

Whipped cream that comes in aerosol spray cans is much sweeter than the cream you would whip yourself. Also, there is more air than cream, so you are paying a premium for the spray convenience. When you whip your own cream, you will get a lot more flavour, no additives, and a healthier end product.

Indian Pudding with Whipped Cream

*If you make too much, let it firm up and fry it in butter,
making sweet griddle cakes for breakfast the next day.*

1. Preheat the oven to 120°C/250°F/Gas ½. Heat half the milk. Place the cornmeal and the rest of the dry ingredients, the ginger and treacle in the top of a double boiler.

2. Whisk the hot milk into the mixture, cooking and stirring over simmering water for 10 minutes or until smooth. Butter a pie dish.

3. Whisk the remaining, cold, milk into the hot mixture and pour into the baking dish. Bake for 3 hours. Serve hot or at room temperature with whipped cream.

Serves 8

4 cups milk
¼ cup cornmeal
⅓ cup dark brown sugar
¼ cup white sugar
1 teaspoon salt
1 teaspoon cinnamon
¼ teaspoon ground nutmeg
1 teaspoon chopped fresh
    ginger
¼ cup black treacle
5 tablespoons unsalted butter

Swedish Fruit Pudding (Kram)

*Children and adults like this equally well. It's tangy and very bright red.
Serve it in wineglasses with a spoonful of whipped cream on top.*

1. Place the thawed berries in a saucepan. Drain off the juice produced from thawing into a bowl. Mix in the lemon juice. Add the arrowroot or cornflour to the mixture.

2. Stir the liquid and a pinch of salt into the berries. Cook over a low heat until the mixture starts to thicken. Add the liqueur. Cool and serve in wineglasses with whipped cream.

Serves 4

10oz frozen strawberries
10oz frozen raspberries
¼ cup lemon juice
1½ tablespoons arrowroot
    or cornflour
Pinch salt
¼ cup sugar, or to taste
2 tablespoons orange liqueur
    (optional)
Whipped cream or ice cream

Kram with Cranberries

A variation on the traditional Scandinavian pudding.

Serves 4

14oz cranberries
½ cup sugar or to taste
3 tablespoons cornflour or
    arrowroot
½ cup cold water
1 cup double cream whipped
    with 1 teaspoon sugar

1. Place the berries and sugar in a saucepan.

2. Mix the cornflour with cold water in a separate cup until smooth. Add to the berries.

3. Simmer over a low heat until the mixture thickens. Cool. Whip the cream and add to the berry mixture.

Plum Parfait

This is really easy, and pretty. But you must have fresh, large, sweet plums. Skip it if the plums are wizened or small.

Serves 4

1½ teaspoons powdered
    gelatine
2 tablespoons water
½ cup sugar, or to taste
4 purple or red plums
1 cup water
1in strip orange rind
1 cup double cream, whipped
    with 1 tablespoon sugar

1. In a blender, sprinkle the gelatine over the cold water. Leave until the gelatine 'blooms'.

2. In a saucepan, mix the sugar, plums, orange rind, and water; bring to a boil. Pour the sugar/water over the gelatine and blend. When the plums are cool enough to handle, remove the pits and add the fruit to the blender, skin and all.

3. Spoon cooled plum mixture into wineglasses, making layers with the whipped cream. Swirl with a knife. Chill and serve.

Panna Cotta

This classic Italian dessert has multiple variations – you can make it with cream, milk, yogurt or buttermilk, or a mixture of these four.

Serves 6

2 teaspoons water
2 teaspoons powdered
   gelatine
1 cup whipping cream
⅓ cup sugar, or to taste
2 cups buttermilk, well
   shaken
1 teaspoon vanilla
Fruit coulis or fresh fruit of
   your choice

1. Mix the water and gelatine together and leave until the gelatine 'blooms', about 5 minutes.

2. Stir the cream and sugar in a saucepan over moderate heat until the sugar dissolves. Do not boil. Whisk in the gelatine and water; cool to room temperature. Whisk in the buttermilk and vanilla.

3. Lightly oil six 6oz ramekins. Divide the custard between the ramekins. Refrigerate for 6 hours or overnight.

4. Run a sharp knife around the edge of each ramekin. Invert on chilled plates. Serve with fruit coulis or fresh berries or both.

Panna Cotta Flan Custard

Panna cotta, the Italian custard dessert, is basically a custard made with buttermilk. Spanish flan is also a custard and may be made with fruit. Custard is made with eggs, milk, sugar and flavouring. Simple and easy to digest, these custards are basics for adults and children.

Strawberry Clouds

Serves 4

1 ¼oz sachet powdered
   gelatine
¼ cup cold water
1 cup boiling water
8oz strawberries, hulled
Sugar to taste
2 egg whites, stiffly beaten
½ cup double cream,
   whipped with 1
   tablespoon sugar

*These fluffy delights are cool and refreshing. Garnish with sprigs of mint.
The recipe is a cross between a Bavarian cream and a mousse.*

1. Place the gelatine and water in a blender. Leave to stand for 5 minutes so the gelatine can 'bloom'. With the motor running, slowly pour in the boiling water.

2. Add the strawberries and sugar, and whizz until smooth, stopping to scrape down the sides of the goblet.

3. When the berries have cooled, fold in the egg whites and whipped cream. Refrigerate until chilled, mixing occasionally.

Clouds

You can use any berries as a flavouring for clouds, but peaches, blanched and mashed, are also very good, as are pears. Try making a cloud with fresh, spicy apple sauce in autumn. The basic principle works with all fruits. Just vary the amount of sugar to suit the type of fruit; that is, if the fruit is very sweet, use less sugar.

Lemon Clouds

Cool and delicious – this is a delight, any time of year.

1. In a blender, sprinkle the gelatine over the water. Leave to rest for 4–5 minutes. Add the lemon juice, lemon rind, sugar, boiling water and butter. Blend until well mixed. Cool.

2. Beat the egg whites until stiff. Fold them into the lemon mixture. Chill in the refrigerator, stirring every half hour. Place in individual glasses or bowls. Serve with lots of fresh berries.

Serves 4–6

1½ teaspoons powdered gelatine
2 tablespoons cool water
Juice of 1 lemon
1 tablespoon grated lemon rind
½ cup sugar, or to taste
1 cup boiling water
2 tablespoons unsalted butter
4 egg whites

Hot Butter Pecan Sauce

This couldn't be richer or lovelier over ice cream, sorbet or crêpes. Nuts add a wonderful crunch.

Combine the sugars and salt in a heavy-bottomed saucepan. Heat, stirring, until the sugars melt; bring to the boil. Cook over a high heat until caramelized. Remove from the heat and add the vanilla and cream. Add the nuts, stir, and serve hot.

Makes 1 cup

½ cup dark brown sugar
½ cup white sugar
Pinch salt
1 teaspoon vanilla
¼ cup double cream
1 cup pecan pieces

Chocolate Mousse

The classic darling of the French bistro, this is a fresh take on an old favourite.

Serves 6–8

6oz dark chocolate
¼ cup rum or cognac
½ cup sugar, or to taste
1 teaspoon instant coffee powder
¼ cup boiling water
5 eggs, separated
1 cup double cream, whipped stiff with 1 tablespoon sugar

1. Combine the chocolate, rum or cognac, and sugar in a heavy saucepan or the top of a double boiler. Mix the coffee powder with boiling water and add to the chocolate mixture.

2. Cook over a very low heat, stirring from time to time, until the chocolate melts. Remove from the heat and cool for 3 minutes. Slowly beat in the egg yolks, one at a time.

3. Leave to cool and fold in the egg whites. Spoon into a serving bowl or dessert glasses. Chill for 4–6 hours. Serve with whipped cream.

Garnishes for Chocolate Mousse

Fresh raspberries are a perfect garnish for chocolate mousse, as are sprigs of mint. You can also pour a bit of peppermint schnapps over each serving for an added kick. Chambord (French raspberry liqueur) is also good added to the mousse when you are making it.

Chocolate-Raspberry Soufflé

Chocolate and raspberries are a heavenly combination. Serving a soufflé is grand enough, but adding fresh raspberries to the mix is very special.

Serves 4

3oz bitter chocolate
½ cup sugar
*1 tablespoon butter plus
    1 tablespoon for
    soufflé dish*
*2 tablespoons Chambord
    (raspberry liqueur)*
*3 tablespoons rice flour or
    cornflour*
3 tablespoons cold milk
4 egg yolks
5 egg whites
Pinch cream of tartar
*Fresh raspberries and
    whipped cream to serve*

1. Preheat the oven to 190°C/375°F/Gas 5.

2. In a medium-sized, heavy saucepan, melt the chocolate with the sugar, butter, and Chambord. Remove from the heat. Whisk the flour and milk together and add to the chocolate mixture.

3. Beat the egg yolks, one at a time, into the chocolate mixture. Whip the egg whites and cream of tartar together until stiff. Fold the egg whites into the chocolate mixture and pour into a buttered 3-pint soufflé dish.

4. Bake for 35–40 minutes or until puffed and brown. Serve with fresh raspberries and whipped cream.

The Creative Soufflé

The variety of soufflés you can make is limited only by the availability of ingredients and your imagination. You can substitute mashed bananas for the chocolate, or mangos, for that matter. The soufflé makes a marvellous entrance, but it must be served immediately or it will flop.

Espresso Custard

This silky, rich custard can be served with whipped cream or coffee ice cream.

Serves 4

3 tablespoons instant
   espresso powder
2 tablespoons boiling water
2 cups whipping cream
3 whole eggs
4 teaspoons cornflour
4 teaspoons cold water
½ cup sugar, or to taste
1 teaspoon vanilla

1. Preheat oven to 160°C/325°F/Gas 3. Whisk together the espresso powder and boiling water, add the cream, and beat in the eggs. Whisk the cornflour and water together until smooth and beat into the mixture.

2. Add the rest of the ingredients and stir well. Place four buttered 6oz ramekins in a roasting tin of hot water. Pour in the custard.

3. Bake in the centre of the oven for 50–60 minutes. Serve warm, at room temperature, or chilled with whipped cream.

Espresso

Espresso coffee beans are roasted longer than beans for regular coffee, that's why they have such a dark and deep flavour. In cooking, use instant espresso powder, and you certainly can use decaf espresso powder for equally good results, with no caffeine buzz.

Half-Frozen Mocha Mousse

Mocha, the combination of coffee and chocolate, is said to be an aphrodisiac. And when it's frozen enough to be icy cold and very dark, it could evoke Eros.

෯෩

1. Blend the espresso powder, cocoa powder and water together until smooth. Add sugar, vanilla and salt.

2. Whip the cream and fold the cocoa mixture into it, mixing gently but thoroughly.

3. Place in a bowl in the freezer for 1 hour, stirring occasionally; do not freeze hard. Serve in balloon wineglasses with shaved chocolate sprinkled over the top.

Serves 4

2 tablespoons espresso powder
4 tablespoons cocoa powder
⅓ cup iced water
⅔ cup sugar
1 teaspoon vanilla
½ teaspoon salt
1 cup double cream

Pumpkin Custard

You can substitute butternut squash for the pumpkin with good results. Canned pumpkin is very heavy and strong, so try to avoid it.

෯෩

1. Preheat the oven to 160°C/325°F/Gas 3. Purée the pumpkin or squash in a blender or food processor. Slowly add the rest of the ingredients.

2. Pour into a buttered casserole dish. Put the bowl of pumpkin custard in a roasting tin of hot water and bake in the centre of the oven for 50–60 minutes. A nice variation is to add a cup of pecan pieces and let them bake in the custard.

Serves 6–8

2 cups cubed fresh pumpkin or butternut squash, steamed in 1 cup water
½ cup brown sugar
¼ cup white sugar
½ teaspoon each: ground ginger, ground cloves, ground nutmeg
1 teaspoon ground cinnamon
3 eggs, beaten
1 cup double cream

Rice Pudding with Apricots

Serves 6–8

1 cup dried apricots, cut into
     quarters
1 cup water
½ cup sugar
1 cup rice (basmati is
     preferable)
2½ cups milk
1 teaspoon vanilla
⅛ teaspoon nutmeg
½ cup sugar, more to taste
1 cup double cream, whipped
     stiff
4oz blanched almonds,
     toasted

*A classic American idea is to mix canned cherries in heavy syrup with
rice pudding. This is a bit different and, we think, better.*

1. Bring the apricots, water and sugar to the boil and turn down the heat. Simmer until the apricots are plump and the sauce syrupy.

2. In a large, heavy pot, mix the rice and milk. Bring to the boil and then lower the heat to a simmer and cook for about 60 minutes, stirring occasionally.

3. Add the vanilla, nutmeg and sugar, stirring. Cool slightly. Whip the cream and fold it into the pudding. Fold the apricots into the pudding. Top with toasted almonds.

Chocolate Sauce

Makes 1 cup

2oz dark chocolate
½ cup water
½ cup sugar, or to taste
1 teaspoon vanilla extract
2 tablespoons unsalted butter
¼ teaspoon salt

*An essential topping for ice cream, rice pudding and other desserts.
This sauce will keep, refrigerated, for 2 weeks or longer.*

Combine all the ingredients in a heavy saucepan. Cook, stirring, until the sauce is thickened and the sugar is dissolved. Store the sauce in a jar in the refrigerator.

Chapter 17
Kids' Snacks That Parents Love

Popcorn with Spicy Butter

Serves 2

4oz butter or margarine
1 teaspoon Tabasco sauce
½ teaspoon freshly ground
   black pepper
1 teaspoon salt
1 pack microwave popcorn
   or 4 cups popped
   corn, unflavoured and
   unbuttered

*This is an excellent change from regular buttered popcorn.
You can add more heat to it if you like, as well as seasoned salt.*

Melt the butter and add seasonings. Pour over hot popcorn, mixing vigorously.

Roasted Pink Pepper Nuts

Makes 2½ cups

4oz unsalted butter
¾ cup brown sugar
4 teaspoons water
½ teaspoon ground cloves
¼ teaspoon cinnamon
2 teaspoons salt
1 tablespoon freshly ground
   pink peppercorns
2½ cups blanched almonds

*These will keep in an airtight container. You can also substitute
black or white pepper with only slightly different results.*

1. Preheat the oven to 180°C/350°F/Gas 4. Line a baking sheet with baking parchment.

2. Melt the butter. Add the sugar and water and mix, stirring, over a medium heat. Add the spices, salt and pepper. When well blended, add the almonds and stir to coat.

3. Transfer the nuts to the baking sheet. Bake for about 10 minutes, until well browned. Cool and store in airtight container.

Crunchy Cornbread Squares

These can also be cut into rectangles and used as bases for dips and spreads.

Makes 15–20 squares

1 cup cornmeal
1 cup maize flour (masa harina)
2 teaspoons bicarbonate of soda
1 teaspoon cream of tartar
1 teaspoon salt, or to taste
4 tablespoons white or brown sugar
1 cup sour cream
¼ cup buttermilk
2 beaten eggs
4 tablespoons butter, melted

1. Grease and line a 9 x 13in baking tin and preheat the oven to 220°C/425°F/Gas 7. Mix all the dry ingredients together in a bowl. Stir in the sour cream, buttermilk and eggs. (You can add various herbs and spices to change the flavours, such as oregano and garlic powder for an Italian flavour, or chilli and cumin for a Mexican taste.)

2. Pour into the prepared tin and bake for 20 minutes or until lightly browned.

Snacking

An inevitable part of most people's eating habits, snacks should be a healthy addition to the diet. Sugary snacks such as cakes and sweets are not all that helpful, as they produce a sugar high followed by more hunger. Real food is satisfying and keeps away hunger.

Chilli Bean Dip with Dipping Vegetables

Makes 2 pints

½lb ground beef
1 onion, chopped
2 jalapeño chillis, or to taste,
    cored, seeded
    and chopped
2 cloves garlic, chopped
¼ cup vegetable oil
4 teaspoons chilli powder, or
    to taste
1 14oz can chopped tomatoes
    with juice
1 14oz can red kidney beans
½ cup flat gluten-free beer
assortment of carrots,
    celery sticks, radishes,
    broccoli florets, courgette
    sticks etc

This is a great way to get kids eating vegetables, and makes a substantial snack for after school. Serve with Crunchy Cornbread Squares (page 239).

1. Sauté the beef and vegetables in the oil, breaking up with a spoon to avoid clumping.

2. When the vegetables are soft, add the rest of the ingredients (except the vegetables for dipping). Cover and simmer for 1 hour. To turn it into a dip, cool a little and pulse it in the food processor. Do not make it smooth. Serve alongside veggies.

Chilli and Beans

There are endless variations of the chilli and bean combination. Some people use turkey, others add dark chocolate and cinnamon and vary the amounts of spice, beans and tomatoes. Some forms of chilli don't have any beans.

Hot and Sweet Peppers with Jack Cheese Stuffing

This is an easy snack or cocktail nibble.

1. Preheat the oven to 180°C/350°F/Gas 4.

2. Grease a baking dish and lay the peppers in the dish. Drizzle them with olive oil. Divide the cheese among the peppers.

3. Mix the cornbread crumbs, pepper, cayenne and Parmesan together and spoon over the cheese in the peppers. Bake until the cheese melts, about 10 minutes. Serve garnished with shredded lettuce and a dollop of sour cream.

Serves 4

4 red peppers, cut in quarters, cored and seeded
4 teaspoons olive oil
4oz Monterey jack or Gruyère cheese, shredded
½ cup Crunchy Cornbread Squares (see page 239), crumbled in the blender or food processor
Freshly ground black pepper and cayenne to taste
4 teaspoons grated Parmesan cheese for topping
Shredded lettuce and sour cream, for garnish

Peppers with Jalapeño Jelly and Cream Cheese Stuffing

This can also be served on gluten-free crackers or Crunchy Cornbread Squares (see page 239). The combination of sweet, hot and creamy is irresistible.

Arrange the cut pepper 'spoons' on a platter. Place a dab of cream cheese on each, add a dab of the hot/sweet jalapeño jelly, and serve.

Makes 32 pieces

4 large, ripe red peppers, cored, seeded, cut into quarters and then halved
8oz cream cheese
1 8oz jar jalapeño jelly or other sweet chilli relish

Devilled Eggs with Caviar or Prawns

*There is nothing more delightful than a devilled egg with
a dab of caviar on top and a dab of sour cream on top of that.*

Makes 10

5 hard-boiled eggs
½ cup whole or low-fat
  mayonnaise
1 teaspoon Dijon mustard
1 teaspoon Tabasco sauce or
  other hot pepper sauce
½ bunch of chives, snipped
  finely
2 teaspoons capers, the
  smallest available
2oz red salmon caviar or 10
  small cooked prawns
Sour cream if you are using
  caviar

1. Peel the eggs, cut them in half, and remove the yolks to the food processor. Arrange the whites on a platter.

2. Add the mayonnaise, mustard, pepper sauce, chives and capers to the food processor and blend.

3. Stuff the egg whites with the yolk mixture and place ¼ teaspoon caviar on top of each, or a small prawns. Serve with sour cream on the side to go with the caviar.

Olive Oil in Spray Bottles

This is a very easy and economical way to use olive oil. Just buy a bottle used for spraying plants with water and fill it with olive oil. Use it for spraying food or to lightly oil pans and grills before use.

Barbecued Curried Chicken Wings

These spicy grilled wings are a lot less fattening than fried chicken. Double the quantity and refrigerate half for delicious cold snacks.

1. Rinse the wings and set them on paper towels to dry.

2. In a large bowl, mix the rest of the ingredients together. Coat the chicken with the curry mixture, cover, and refrigerate for 1 hour.

3. Barbecue over medium-hot coals or grill at 180°C/350°F for 20 minutes, turning every few minutes, or until well browned.

Serves 4–8

4lb chicken wings, split at the joint, tips removed
1 tablespoon curry powder, or to taste
1 tablespoon onion powder
1 tablespoon garlic powder
¼ teaspoon cinnamon
2 teaspoons dark brown sugar
¼ cup freshly squeezed lime juice
¼ cup olive oil
1 teaspoon salt
Ground black pepper to taste

Fiery Barbecued Chicken Wings

The really great part about this recipe is that you can make it as hot as you please. For kids, it's better to use just a bit of heat, not too much.

1. Rinse the chicken and pat dry with paper towels. (If the chicken is wet, the coating won't stick to it.)

2. Mix the butter, Tabasco and salt in a bowl. Turn the chicken pieces in the bowl to coat.

3. Barbecue over a medium heat or grill at 180°C/350°F until the chicken is browned and sizzling, about 20 minutes. Be careful not to burn it. Serve with celery and blue cheese dressing.

Serves 4–8

4lb chicken wings, split at joint, tips removed
½lb butter, melted
4–8 teaspoons Tabasco or other hot pepper sauce
1–2 teaspoons salt, or to taste
Garnish of celery sticks with blue cheese dressing

Stuffed Celery with
Gorgonzola and Green Peppercorns

Makes 1½ cups

1 bunch celery, washed and
   cut into 2in lengths
¾ cup sour cream
½ cup crumbled Gorgonzola
   cheese
1 tablespoon lemon juice
1 tablespoon chopped onion
1 teaspoon celery salt
1 teaspoon Tabasco or other
   hot pepper sauce
2 tablespoons green
   peppercorns, in brine
Garnishes of your choice

*Celery is a great replacement for – not to mention healthier than –
crackers when you are on a gluten-free diet.*

1. Arrange the celery on a platter, cover and refrigerate.

2. Mix the rest of the ingredients together. Stuff the celery and serve. You can put this together 2–3 hours in advance.

3. Garnish with chopped chives, small prawns, pieces of roasted red pepper, halved black olives and/or herbs such as parsley, chives or oregano.

Pork Spare Ribs

Serves 4–6

4lb pork spare ribs, cut into
   1-rib pieces
½ cup vegetable oil
1 cup of your favourite
   barbecue sauce
1 cup tomato juice
½ cup orange juice

*You can use Chinese or any kind of barbecue sauce you wish.
The trick is to cook the ribs in the sauce.*

1. Fry the ribs in vegetable oil, turning, over a medium-high heat until lightly brown.

2. Add the rest of the ingredients and cover. Cook over a very low heat for 1 hour.

3. Remove the ribs and continue cooking the sauce until reduced to 1 cup. Serve the sauce with the ribs for dipping.

Grilled Cheese on Toasted Cornbread Squares

*This recipe is one of the hundreds of goodies you can make if you have
Crunchy Cornbread Squares in your fridge or freezer.*

Makes 32 small squares

*1 recipe Crunchy Cornbread
    Squares (see page 239)*
½ cup soft butter
*1 cup cubed Monterey jack or
    Gruyère cheese*
*½ cup grated Parmesan
    cheese*
*½ cup red roasted peppers,
    (from a jar is fine)*
*½ cup chopped sweet red
    onion*

1. Arrange the cornbread squares on an oiled baking sheet. Preheat the
    oven to 180°C/350°F/Gas 4.

2. Whizz the rest of the ingredients in a food processor until mixed. Don't
    worry about making the cheese mixture smooth. Using a teaspoon,
    place a small mound of the mixture on each cornbread square.

3. Bake until the cheese melts, about 10 minutes. You can vary this recipe by
    adding different herbs, chopped garlic or any of your favourite flavours.

Stuffings and Spreads

*Making spreads and stuffings for any number of things is a great way to use left-
overs. You can take a chunk of leftover Brie cheese and put it in the food processor
with some chopped onion and a bit of butter or margarine and have a whole new
experience. Leftover chicken is excellent for making many different spreads, filling
for stuffed celery, or a little sandwich.*

Chickpea Crêpes for Stuffing

1¼ cups cold water
1 egg
1 teaspoon Tabasco or other
   hot pepper sauce
1 cup chickpea flour
1 teaspoon salt
1 teaspoon garlic powder
   (optional)
Vegetable or olive oil for
   frying

*These are so versatile – you can stuff and fold them or roll and stuff them,
as you would cannelloni or manicotti, for a main course.*

1. Place the water, egg and Tabasco in a blender or food processor. Whizz, slowly adding the flour. Stop and scrape down the sides.

2. Blend in the salt and garlic powder. Heat a nonstick pan over a medium-high heat and add a teaspoon of olive or vegetable oil.

3. Pour about 2 tablespoons of batter into the pan, tipping it quickly to spread the batter. Fry for about 3 minutes or until the edges are crisp. Flip carefully, and when golden, place on greaseproof paper or baking parchment to cool.

4. Fold or form into tubes. Stuff with fillings from this chapter.

Crêpes – a Taste of Elegance

The great thing about all crêpes is that they add a touch of elegance and charm to any meal or snack offering. The second great thing is that crêpes can be made in advance and then refrigerated or frozen. They are wonderful to have on hand – if unexpected guests show up for cocktails and supper, well, you're all set. The only pieces of equipment required are a blender and a nonstick frying pan.

Hot Hot Dogs

This is a really great way to serve hot dogs to people on a gluten-free diet.
Turning them into a spread is an exciting twist.

1. Oil a baking sheet. Preheat the oven to 180°C/350°F/Gas 4.

2. Mix the hot dogs, mustard, onion and relish in a food processor.

3. Spread a teaspoon of the mixture on one quarter of each crêpe and fold in half, then in quarters.

4. Bake for about 10 minutes, until hot. Serve with plenty of mustard on the side.

Serves 6–8

3 frankfurters, barbecued, grilled or boiled
2 teaspoons Dijon mustard
2 teaspoons chopped onion
2 teaspoons cucumber or tomato relish
1 recipe Chickpea Crêpes (see page 246)

Curried Chicken

This whole concept is very Middle Eastern. This is to be stuffed in crêpes.

1. Stack the crêpes with greaseproof paper between them. Mix together the chicken, curry powder and chutney. Place a spoonful of the chicken curry mixture on a quarter section of each crêpe.

2. Fold in quarters. Place on a platter and serve.

Serves 8

1 recipe Chickpea Crepes (see page 246)
½lb chicken breast, poached for 10 minutes, or leftover cooked chicken, chopped
½ cup plain yogurt
2 teaspoons curry powder, or to taste
¼ cup mango chutney

Peanut Butter, Banana and Bacon Stuffing

Makes 8–10 small crêpes

1 slice banana per crêpe
8 half-teaspoons peanut
butter
1 recipe Chickpea Crêpes (see
page 246)
8 half-teaspoons honey
4 rashers streaky bacon, fried
crisp and crumbled

*This is perfect as an after-school snack for kids on the go.
It's also comfort food for grownups.*

Place the banana and peanut butter next to each other on one end of a crêpe. Drizzle with honey and sprinkle with crumbled bacon. Fold the peanut butter, honey and bacon side over the banana and fold again.

Pepperoni and Cheese Stuffing

Makes 8–10 crêpes

2oz fresh mozzarella cheese,
cut in small pieces
8–10 slices pepperoni
1 recipe Chickpea Crêpes
(small, about 4in across;
see page 246)

*This is another tasty idea for stuffing crêpes. You can add some roasted red
pepper, onion, or a teaspoon of canned chopped tomato.*

1. Oil a baking sheet. Place some cheese and pepperoni on a quarter of each crêpe. Add anything else you've decided on. If desired, you can place a drop of pizza sauce on each crêpe just before folding.

2. Bake until the cheese melts, about 10 minutes.

Chapter 18

A Dinner Party Buffet for Twelve

Fried Polenta Squares with Salsa

Make the polenta a day in advance,
then refrigerate it until just before the party.

Makes 12–24 squares

6½ cups of water
2 tablespoons salt
2 cups cornmeal
2–4oz unsalted butter
2 tablespoons dried herbs
 or 1 tablespoon each
 fresh basil, rosemary
 and parsley
½ cup freshly grated
 Parmesan cheese
Freshly ground black pepper
 to taste
2 tablespoons unsalted butter
 and 2–4 tablespoons
 vegetable oil, for frying
1 8oz jar of your favourite
 salsa or homemade
 Guacamole (see page
 251) for dipping

1. Bring the water to the boil.

2. Add salt, and using your hand, drop the cornmeal into the boiling water, letting it slip slowly between your fingers to make a very slim stream. You should be able to see each grain. Do not dump the cornmeal into the water or you will get a mass of glue.

3. Stir constantly while adding the cornmeal. Reduce the heat to a simmer and keep stirring for about 20 minutes as it thickens.

4. Stir in the butter, herbs, Parmesan cheese and pepper. Spread in an oiled 9 x 13in glass dish.

5. Chill for 3 hours or overnight. Cut into squares and fry until golden brown over medium heat in a combination of butter and oil. If you are having an outdoor party, you can barbecue the squares over a low flame for a smoky flavour. Serve with salsa or guacamole.

Guacamole

There are many recipes for guacamole. Some employ smoked chillis, others use tomatoes, and yet others combine lemon and lime juice.

Using a fork, mash the avocados, mixing in the rest of the ingredients until well blended.

Choosing Avocados

Most store-bought avocados are as hard as stones. That's fine; if you buy ripe ones, they generally have many blemishes. Just buy them a few days before you plan to serve them. Place them on a sunny windowsill or in a brown paper bag or wrap them in a newspaper. The paper seems to hasten ripening. The avocado should not have oily black spots in it when you cut it open but should be a uniform green. One or two black spots can be cut out, but don't use an avocado that is full of black spots or grey-brown areas.

Makes 1–1½ cups

3 medium Hass avocados or
   2 large, smooth-skinned
   ones, peeled and seeded
Juice of 2 limes
½ cup finely chopped sweet
   onion
1 teaspoon Tabasco sauce, or
   to taste
½ teaspoon salt, or to taste
2 tablespoons finely chopped
   fresh coriander

Gravlax (Salmon Cured in Sugar and Salt)

This is a year-round Swedish speciality – good on any buffet at any special occasion. The salmon will 'cook' or 'cure' in the salt and sugar.

Serves 12–15

3lb side of salmon, skin removed
⅔ cup salt
½ cup granulated sugar
20 white peppercorns, crushed
6 thick slices fresh ginger, peeled
5 large fronds fresh dill
1 recipe Cucumber Sauce (see below)
1 recipe Mustard Sauce (see page 253)

1. Rinse the salmon and dry on paper towels.

2. In a large glass dish, mix together the salt, sugar and pepper. Place the salmon in the dish and turn it to cover with the mixture.

3. Arrange the ginger over and under the fish. Place fronds of dill over and under the fish. Cover tightly and refrigerate for 16–24 hours.

4. Scrape off the salt and sugar, wiping the fish with paper towels. Slice thinly, on the diagonal, and serve with sprigs of watercress, hard-boiled egg slices and the dressings.

Cucumber Sauce for Gravlax

*This is such a great accompaniment for Gravlax.
It's also good with cold roast beef, roasted beef fillet or ham.*

Makes 3 cups

1 long cucumber, peeled
1 red onion, chopped finely
1½ cups sour cream
½ cup chopped fresh dill
Juice and grated zest of 1 lemon
1 teaspoon champagne vinegar or other white wine vinegar
1 teaspoon salt
Black or white pepper, freshly ground, to taste
Chopped chives and parsley for garnish

1. Slice the cucumber in half lengthwise and scoop out the seeds and discard. Chop the cucumber finely.

2. Add the rest of the ingredients, except the chives and parsley. Leave the sauce in the refrigerator for at least 2 hours to 'marry' and bring out the flavours of the ingredients.

3. Garnish with chives and parsley. Serve the sauce in a chilled bowl alongside the gravlax.

Mustard Sauce for Gravlax, Ham or Roast Beef

*This is so simple and good, you won't ever go wrong making it.
You can also serve it with salads.*

Makes 1 cup

2/3 cup olive oil
1/3 cup white wine vinegar
1 tablespoon Dijon mustard
1 teaspoon sugar
Salt and pepper to taste
Fresh herbs such as dill,
    oregano, parsley or basil

Place all the ingredients in a blender and whizz until emulsified. Serve in a glass bowl or sauceboat. Store in a glass jar, covered, in the refrigerator. It will keep for a week, depending on the freshness of the herbs. It will keep longer if you have used dried herbs.

Hot or Cold Asparagus Soup

*Small cups of this served icy cold on a hot day, or warm and creamy on
a cold day, are welcome. You can also garnish it with small cooked prawns.*

Serves 12–15

4 shallots, chopped
2 tablespoons olive oil
2lb fresh asparagus, cut into
    1in pieces
4 pints chicken stock
Salt and pepper to taste
Juice of 1 lemon, and 1
    teaspoon grated
    lemon zest
1 teaspoon Tabasco sauce,
    or to taste
2 cups double cream
1/2 cup chopped fresh chives
    or mint leaves, for garnish

1. In a large, heavy-bottomed saucepan, sauté the shallots in olive oil. When they are softened, add the asparagus and toss for a few minutes.

2. Add the stock, salt, pepper, lemon juice and zest and Tabasco. Cover and cook until the asparagus is very tender.

3. Whizz in the blender until very smooth. If you are going to serve it hot, reheat, add cream, and serve. For a cold soup, chill, add cream, and serve. Garnish with chopped fresh chives or mint leaves.

Tiny Chickpea Crêpes

Serves 12 as an appetizer

2 cups chickpea flour
2 cloves garlic, crushed
1 teaspoon Tabasco sauce or
    other hot sauce
1 teaspoon salt or to taste
1½ cups water
Olive oil as needed for
    cooking the crêpes

*These have a nutty flavour that really works with lots of dips and fillings.
You can make them in various sizes, depending on your party size.*

1. Mix everything but the oil in a blender, pulsing and scraping down the side of the jar.

2. Heat some oil in a nonstick pan. Add 1 tablespoon of the batter to make 1½in crêpes.

3. Cook until very crisp on the bottom; do not turn. Remove from the heat and keep on paper towels or a platter. Now you can add fillings of your choice and close, or fold in halves and dip into a sauce.

Rich in Soluble Fibre

Nutritionists say chickpeas are rich in soluble fibre, which is the best type of fibre, actually helping to eliminate cholesterol from the body. Chickpeas are also a good source of folate, vitamin E, potassium, iron, manganese, copper, zinc and calcium. As a high-potassium, low-sodium food, they help reduce blood pressure.

Cheese Fondue with Dipping Vegetables

This can be served as an 'interactive' party appetizer or as a main course.

1. Mash the garlic, and in a large flameproof casserole or fondue dish over a burner, heat the garlic in the wine.

2. Stir in the cheese, nutmeg, pepper, kirsch and salt. Mix and heat slowly over a low flame.

3. In a separate bowl, whisk together the egg yolks, flour and cream. Stir into the cheese mixture and heat gently over a low flame.

4. When the cheese mixture has melted, serve with toasted bread cubes and vegetables, speared on long-handled forks and dipped into the fondue. If the cheese gets too thick, add a bit more warm white wine.

Fondue Facts

Ever wondered where fondue first came from? It was created in Switzerland, where it was a way of using up hardened, stale cheese, and was traditionally a peasant dish. The word comes from the French 'fondre', 'to melt'.

Serves 12–14

1 clove garlic
1 cup dry white wine
1lb Gruyère or Emmental cheese, coarsely grated
¼ teaspoon ground nutmeg
Freshly ground pepper to taste
3 tablespoons kirsch
Salt to taste
2 egg yolks, beaten
2 tablespoons gluten-free flour, such as potato flour
½ cup cream
2 tablespoons butter
1 loaf gluten-free French-style bread, cubed and toasted
1 broccoli crown, blanched in boiling water for 2 minutes, cooled and cut in pieces
2 red peppers, cored, seeded, and cut into chunks
½lb sugar snap peas
2 courgettes and/or 12 very thin asparagus spears, cut up

Grilled Aubergine and Pepper Salad

Serves 12

⅓ cup balsamic or red wine vinegar

1 cup olive oil

1 teaspoon Dijon mustard

Salt and pepper to taste

1 large aubergine, peeled and sliced in ½in rounds

3 red peppers, cored and seeded, cut in half

1 bunch rocket or watercress, stems removed

1 large head romaine lettuce, shredded

4 ripe tomatoes, cored and chopped

2oz aged provolone cheese

Grill the aubergine and peppers the day before the party, then, at the last minute, put the vegetables together, shave the provolone, and dress the salad.

1. Prepare the dressing, mix the first four ingredients together in a jar. Shake well. Brush the aubergine slices with salad dressing and grill for 3 minutes on each side. Cool and cut into cubes.

2. Grill the peppers on the skin side until charred. Place in a paper bag. Cool and pull the skin off. Cut into pieces.

3. Just before serving, toss the salad leaves with the aubergine and peppers, add the tomatoes and shave the provolone over the top.

4. Pour the remaining dressing over the salad.

Paella

You need a really big pan for this – you can get paella pans made of heavy metal that has been coated with enamel.

1. Preheat the oven to 180°C/350°F/Gas 4.

2. Brown the chicken and chorizo in the olive oil and push them to the side of the pan. Add the onion, garlic and rice, stirring to soften the onion and garlic and coat the rice.

3. Add the stock, saffron and tomatoes. Mix well.

4. Bake in the preheated oven for 20 minutes or until the rice begins to take up the stock. Add the peas.

5. The order in which you add the seafood is crucial. Always put in the ones that take the longest to cook first, adding the more tender pieces at the end. Start by arranging the clams on top. When they start to open, add the mussels. When both are open, add the prawns and simply mix them into the rice – they take only 2–3 minutes to cook. Sprinkle with parsley and serve in the cooking pan.

Different Regions, Different Paellas

Different regions of Spain use different ingredients in their paella. Here, in the United States, you may find lobster rather than langostini in paella, and we always use lots of clams.

Serves 10–16

2 chickens, cut into 10 pieces
1lb chorizo, cut into bite-sized
    pieces
½ cup olive oil
1 large onion, diced
2 cloves garlic, chopped
3 cups rice
5½ cups chicken stock
Pinch saffron
2 tomatoes, cored and
    chopped
10oz frozen petit pois
18 clams, scrubbed
18 mussels, scrubbed and
    debearded
1½lb raw jumbo prawns,
    peeled and deveined
½ cup chopped fresh parsley

Stuffed, Roasted Fillet of Beef

This can be served hot, cold or at room temperature.
The garlic and spinach stuffing is a terrific counterpoint to the meat.

Serves 10–12

1lb fresh spinach, blanched, and squeezed to remove extra moisture
2 tablespoons olive oil
4 cloves garlic, chopped
Juice of ½ lemon
¼ teaspoon nutmeg
1 cup gluten-free soft breadcrumbs mixed with seasonings such as dried oregano and salt and pepper to taste
1 6lb beef fillet, well trimmed
1 teaspoon salt and freshly ground black pepper to taste
2 tablespoons softened butter
1 pint fresh beef stock

1. Preheat the oven to 180°C/350°F/Gas 4.

2. Place the spinach on paper towels to dry a bit. Heat the olive oil and add the garlic; cook over a medium heat to soften. Mix in the spinach, lemon juice and nutmeg, stirring. Add the breadcrumbs.

3. Using a fat knitting needle or the handle of a dull knife, make a channel through the meat. Force in the stuffing.

4. Sprinkle the meat with salt and pepper, then rub with the softened butter. Roast for 60 minutes, basting every 15 minutes with the beef stock. Reserve the pan juices for another use. Let the fillet rest for 15 minutes before serving.

Alternatives to Breadcrumbs

Try using your food processor to make crumbs of such goodies as cornbread, potato crisps or popcorn. Check various rice cereals such as puffed rice and rice crispies to make sure they are gluten-free, then put them in the processor to make crumbs. Store the crumbs in sealed plastic bags in the refrigerator.

Chocolate-Dipped Strawberries

*This crowd-pleaser is always delicious and is good to make in advance.
Buy the best strawberries you can find.*

Makes 36 berries

*36 very large strawberries
with long stems
8oz bitter chocolate
6oz milk chocolate
4oz sugar*

1. Rinse the berries and allow them to dry on paper towels.

2. Melt the chocolate and sugar in a double boiler over simmering water. Remove from the heat.

3. Carefully dip the strawberries, one at a time, in the chocolate. Store in a cool place, or if made more than 5 hours ahead of time, store in the refrigerator.

A Valentine's Treat

One of the most popular Valentine's Day gifts is chocolate-dipped strawberries, with their bloom of red along with creamy or dark chocolate. Surprise your loved one with a homemade rendition that will melt his or her heart.

Dark Chocolate, Walnut and Hazelnut Torte

Serves 14

1lb bitter chocolate, chopped
1 cup unsalted butter, cut into pieces
¼ cup cocoa powder
¼ cup hazelnut liqueur
½ teaspoon vanilla extract
5 eggs
2 teaspoons grated orange zest
1 cup hazelnuts, toasted, skinned and ground
1 cup walnuts, toasted and ground
½ cup icing sugar

This is exceedingly rich and delicious. Serve it with coffee or vanilla ice cream. A few fresh raspberries on the side are also an excellent counterpoint.

1. Preheat the oven to 180°C/350°F/Gas 4. In the top of a double boiler, heat the chocolate and butter until the chocolate melts. Remove from the heat and stir.

2. Add the cocoa, liqueur, vanilla, eggs and orange zest, mixing well.

3. Add the hazelnuts and walnuts and mix. Pour the batter into a greased 9in cake tin lined with baking parchment. Bake until the cake is barely set, about 25–30 minutes.

4. Cool in the tin for 20 minutes. Remove from the tin and place on a rack to cool completely.

5. Dust with icing sugar. Serve with raspberries and ice cream.

Vanilla

Whatever you do, don't use imitation vanilla extract – the pure stuff is more expensive, but it tastes so much better it's worth it. Imitation vanilla extract may give food a slight chemical flavour. You can use vanilla pods to make flavoured sugar: simply slit open a pod and place it in a jar with 2 cups sugar, seal and leave for a week.

Chapter 19
A Gluten-Free
Birthday Party for Kids

Raw Veggies with Chilli Cheddar Cheese Dip

Makes 2 cups

Mixed raw vegetables such as
    carrots, celery and green
    and yellow peppers
2 tablespoons butter or
    margarine
2 tablespoons cornflour or
    maize flour (masa harina)
1 cup warm milk
1½ cups grated Cheddar
    cheese
1 tablespoon onion powder
1 tablespoon chilli powder, or
    to taste
1 tablespoon paprika

*This is good for an autumn or winter birthday party; it's fun to eat with
crisp celery, carrots or strips of red pepper. Kids of all ages love it.*

1. Prepare the vegetables and place them in a plastic bag in the refrigerator.

2. Melt the butter and stir in the cornflour or maize flour. Whisk in the milk; cook until thick. Add the rest of the ingredients, stir well, and serve with the veggies.

Raw Veggies with Cheese Dip

Makes 2 cups

4oz cream cheese, at room
    temperature
4oz blue or Gorgonzola
    cheese, at room
    temperature
½ cup mayonnaise
½ cup sour cream
1 teaspoon celery salt
Freshly ground black pepper
    to taste
Platter of raw vegetables

This is great for kids and adults; add spice as your taste buds dictate.

Whizz everything but the vegetables in the food processor, stopping occasionally to scrape the sides of the bowl. Refrigerate or serve immediately. Serve surrounded by veggies.

Going for the Crunch

Everybody loves crunchy foods, especially kids. And when dipped in wonderful hot and/or cold cheese sauces, vegetables are even better. This is a great way to get greens such as raw broccoli, sugar snap peas and spring onions into children. Of course, carrots and celery are standard, but try some red and/or yellow peppers to up the vitamins.

Deep-Fried Chicken Wings

Adjust the quantities to whatever else you are serving and to the size/ages of the kids attending the party. Use 10 to 12 wings for each teenager, and 4 to 5 for each kindergartner.

Makes 20 wings

20 chicken wings, halved and trimmed
1½ cups chickpea flour
1 teaspoon bicarbonate of soda
1 teaspoon garlic powder
1½ cups water
1 egg
Salt and pepper to taste
Vegetable oil for deep frying, about 4 pints

1. Rinse the chicken pieces and dry thoroughly on paper towels.

2. Mix the flour, bicarbonate of soda, garlic powder, water, egg, salt and pepper in the blender until smooth. Pour into a large bowl.

3. Heat the oil to 180°C/350°F. Dip the wings, 3 or 4 at a time, in the batter and, using tongs, place them in the hot oil. Fry for 20 minutes.

4. Drain on paper towels. Keep the wings warm in a low oven if you make them in advance. Serve with hot sauce on the side for older kids.

A Trade Secret

To turn fried wings into Buffalo wings, named after the town in upstate New York, mix ½lb butter, 2 teaspoons cider vinegar and hot sauce to taste in a saucepan over a medium heat. When the butter is melted, dip the wings into the sauce, to heat and flavour them.

Sausages on Quartered Sweet Peppers

*A little sausage goes a long way. Use a mild-flavoured sausage
for young kids; older ones may like a spicier taste.*

Makes 16 pieces

1lb sausages
4 large red or green peppers,
cored, seeded and cut
into quarters

1. Place the whole sausages in a pot with water to cover, then bring to a rolling boil. Reduce the heat and simmer for 10 minutes.

2. Remove the sausages from the water. Grill under a high heat until nicely browned all over. Cut in rounds and serve on 'spoons' of red or green pepper.

Spaghetti Squash with Tomato Sauce and Cheese

Spaghetti squash holds endless possibilities for a nutritious, gluten-free diet. It's delicious and so easy to prepare.

Serves 6–8

1 4lb spaghetti squash
1 cup freshly grated
    Parmesan cheese
Garnish of fresh herbs such
    as parsley, basil, and
    oregano
2 cups of your favorite
    prepared, gluten-free
    tomato sauce

1. Preheat the oven to 140°C/275°F/Gas 1.

2. Make a boat of aluminium foil and place the squash in the centre. Pierce the squash in several places with a knife to let the steam escape. Sprinkle with water. Tent with more foil and roast for 2 hours. The squash is done when you can insert a fork easily.

3. Cool the squash so you can handle it. Cut it in half and scoop out the seeds. Using a fork, run it through the flesh and it will turn into spaghetti.

4. Mix the squash and most of the cheese together and reheat. Sprinkle with the remaining cheese and herbs, toss with the sauce and serve.

Freshly Grated Cheese

Blocks of Parmesan cheese will keep for a week, tightly wrapped, in the refrigerator. It is so easy to grate exactly the amount you need, when you need it, and it tastes 100 per cent better than the cheese you buy ready grated. Use a box grater and place a piece of greaseproof paper on your board. Grate away, then remove the grater, make a funnel of the paper, and slide the cheese into a bowl or add it to what you are preparing.

Spaghetti Squash Macaroni Cheese

Everybody loves macaroni and cheese. This recipe substitutes spaghetti squash for the macaroni and uses Chilli Cheddar Cheese Dip.

Serves 4–6

1 5lb spaghetti squash, rinsed
1 quantity Chilli Cheddar
    Cheese Dip (see page 262)
½ cup milk
1½ cups extra grated Cheddar
    cheese for topping
2 tablespoons butter

1. Preheat the oven to 140°C/275°F/Gas 1.

2. Make a boat of aluminium foil and place the squash in the centre. Pierce the squash in several places with a knife to let the steam escape. Sprinkle with water. Tent with more foil and roast for 2 hours. The squash is done when you can insert a fork easily.

3. Cool the squash so you can handle it. Grease a 10in baking dish. Using a fork, make 'spaghetti' of the squash and scrape it into the dish.

4. Increase the oven temperature to 180°C/350°F/Gas 4.

5. Mix the sauce and extra milk into the squash. Sprinkle the extra cheese on top and dot with butter. Bake for 30 minutes, until the dish is hot and bubbling.

Homemade Potato Crisps

These are just too good and will be grabbed up fast, so plan to make extra.

1. Peel and slice the potatoes. The best way to do this is with a mandolin or the slicing blade on a food processor.

2. Place 2in of oil in the fryer. Heat the oil to 170°C/340°F and watch the temperature throughout the cooking time.

3. Carefully add the potato slices, a few at a time, to the hot oil. Remove when golden and drain on brown paper bags or paper towels. Sprinkle with salt. Serve hot or warm. (For a variation, mix 2 teaspoons chilli powder with 2 teaspoons salt and sprinkle on the crisps as they cool.)

Makes about 75 chips

4 large potatoes
4 pints light vegetable oil, such as canola
Salt to taste

Fresh Three-Berry Granita

This is fine as it is or mixed with vanilla ice cream.
The more varieties of fruit you use, the better.

1. Mix the sugar and water together in a large saucepan and bring to the boil. Reduce the heat and simmer until all the sugar is dissolved.

2. Add the prepared berries and cook for 6 minutes. Add the lemon juice.

3. Place in the freezer in ice trays. Occasionally, break up the granita with a fork so that it does not turn into a block of ice. Or use an ice cream freezer to make the granita. The ice cream freezer will increase the shelf life of the granita, making it a sorbet. Soften slightly before serving.

Makes 2 pints

1½ cups sugar
⅔ cups water
8oz strawberries, hulled
12oz fresh raspberries
4oz fresh blueberries
¼ cup lemon juice

Frozen Bananas Dipped in Chocolate

Kids love these and so do lots of grownups.
They're simple to make, and you can involve the older kids in the dipping.

Serves 10

10 bananas
10 lolly sticks
1lb dark chocolate
2 cups sugar, or to taste
Pinch salt
1 teaspoon pure vanilla
    extract

1. Peel the bananas and insert the lolly sticks. Place the bananas on a baking sheet lined with baking parchment and freeze.

2. Just before serving, melt the chocolate and sugar in a large saucepan. Add the salt and vanilla. Leave to cool until just warm but not hard.

3. Dip the frozen bananas into the chocolate and place on greaseproof paper. The frozen bananas will harden the chocolate and they're ready to eat right away.

Jelly Bean Surprise Ice Cream

This is great for little kids – just say, 'Surprise!' and they're happy.

Makes 6 cups

2 pints vanilla ice cream
1½ cups jelly beans

Partially thaw the ice cream. Mix in the jelly beans. Refreeze and serve.

A President's Passion

Former American president Ronald Reagan was renowned for his love of jelly beans. After the president's death, the Jelly Belly candy company created black ribbons in his memory, made out of jelly beans.

Molten Chocolate Chestnut Cake

*The grownups will love this too. Fill the centre with vanilla ice cream
and sprinkle with chocolate chips or M&Ms.*

Serves 10–12

1 cup chestnut flour
1 cup rice flour
1 tablespoon xanthan gum
¾ cup cocoa powder
2 teaspoons baking powder
Pinch salt
8oz unsalted butter
1¼ cups sugar
1½ cups sour cream
2 eggs
Vanilla or chocolate ice cream
    to fill the centre

1. Preheat the oven to 180°C/350°F/Gas 4. Butter a ring mould and dredge it with rice flour.

2. Sift into a bowl the two flours, xanthan gum, cocoa powder, baking powder and salt.

3. Place the butter and sugar in a large bowl. Using an electric mixer on low speed, mix until creamed and light. Add half the flour/cocoa mixture and beat until well incorporated.

4. Add the sour cream and the eggs and mix vigorously. Slowly add the rest of the flour/cocoa mixture and beat until you are sure there are no lumps.

5. Stop the mixer to scrape the bowl. Pour the batter into the mould and bake for 1 hour. The cake will be soft and custardy. Just before serving, fill with ice cream.

Chocolate and Other Goodies

Chocolate and chestnuts are a marriage made in heaven. Most nuts marry well with chocolate. You could substitute almond flour for chestnut flour in this recipe. Chocolate and coffee are divine together, as are chocolate and raspberries, strawberries or bananas. There's much to be said for combinations of chocolate and vanilla, chocolate and mint, and milk chocolate with dark chocolate. Experiment – you can't go wrong.

Serves 8

3oz bitter chocolate
2oz butter or margarine
1 cup sugar
1 egg
⅔ cup rice flour
1 teaspoon baking powder
1 teaspoon vanilla
2 pints ice cream

Brownie Sundae

*When you crumble warm brownies over
vanilla, chocolate or coffee ice cream, you have something delicious.*

1. Preheat the oven to 150°C/300°F/Gas 2. Line an 8 x 8in baking tin with baking parchment.

2. Melt the chocolate and butter together over a low heat and whisk in the sugar.

3. Mix together the egg, flour, baking powder, and vanilla. Then stir in the chocolate mixture. Pour into the prepared baking tin. Bake for about 30 minutes.

4. Cool for 5 minutes. Crumble and serve over bowls of ice cream.

Chocolate Sauce

When you make a thick chocolate sauce, you need to remember that it is best made with real chocolate, not with cocoa. When you melt the chocolate, you can use a heavy pan or the top of a double boiler. If necessary, add a teaspoon of butter or water to the chocolate.

Appendices

Appendix A:
Keys to a Gluten-Free Diet

Appendix B:
Resources on the Web

Appendix A:
Keys to a Gluten-Free Diet

According to the Gluten Intolerance Group (*www.gluten.net*) and the American Dietetic Association, the following grains, flours, and starches are allowed in a gluten-free diet:

- Buckwheat
- Rice
- Corn
- Potato
- Tapioca
- Bean
- Sorghum
- Soy
- Arrowroot
- Amaranth
- Quinoa
- Millet
- Tef
- Nut

The following grains contain gluten and are not allowed:

- Wheat (durum, semolina)
- Rye
- Barley
- Spelt
- Triticale
- Kamut
- Farina
- Oats

The following ingredients are questionable and should not be consumed unless you can verify that they neither contain nor are derived from prohibited grains:

- Brown rice syrup (frequently made with barley)
- Dextrin (usually corn, but may be derived from wheat)
- Flour or cereal products
- Hydrolyzed vegetable protein (HVP), vegetable protein, hydrolyzed plant protein (HPP), or textured vegetable protein (TVP)
- Malt or malt flavouring (usually made from barley; okay if made from corn)
- Modified food starch or modified starch
- Natural and artificial flavours (However, extracts such as vanilla, orange, and lemon extracts are gluten-free.)

Additional components frequently overlooked that often contain gluten:

- Breading
- Coating mixes
- Communion wafers
- Croutons
- Imitation bacon
- Imitation seafood
- Marinades
- Pastas
- Processed meats
- Roux
- Sauces
- Self-basting poultry
- Soup bases
- Stuffing
- Thickeners

Appendix B:
Resources on the Web

Coeliac UK

www.coeliac.co.uk

This British charity for sufferers from coeliac disease and dermatitis herpetiformis has a membership of around 70,000 and campaigns to improve access to diagnosis, healthcare and safe food. It provides information on health and diet management for sufferers and the food industry.

The George Mateljan Foundation for the World's Healthiest Foods

www.whfoods.com

The George Mateljan Foundation for the World's Healthiest Foods was established by George Mateljan to discover, develop, and share scientifically proven information about the benefits of healthy eating. You can use the site's Recipe Assistant to search for recipes that exclude certain foods.

Juvela

www.juvela.co.uk

A support centre offering advice and information, a regular newsletter, recipes, cookery demonstrations and a range of gluten-free products, which are available in the UK on prescription from pharmacists for sufferers from coeliac disease and dermatitis herpetiformis.

Living Without

www.livingwithout.com

Living Without is a lifestyle guide for people with allergies and food sensitivities. It discusses a wide variety of health issues, including allergies; food sensitivities; multiple chemical sensitivities; wheat intolerance; gluten intolerance; lactose intolerance; dairy allergies; eating disorders; asthma; diabetes; dermatitis; gastroenterology-related disorders; diets that heal; coeliac disease; anaphylaxis; and the common allergens of egg, dairy, wheat, peanuts, tree nuts, shellfish, fish, corn, soy and gluten.

Gluten Freeda

www.glutenfreeda.com

The Glutenfreeda programme was created to help people with coeliac sprue disease learn to prepare all the foods they love, gluten-free. Their goal is to show the gluten-intolerant how to eat well, eat healthily, and how to function happily in a gluten-engorged world. Glutenfreeda recipes will be enjoyed by your entire family and were selected to make eating a delicious experience, not a sacrifice.

Cooking Gluten-Free

www.cookingglutenfree.com

Published by Celiac Publishing, *Cooking Gluten-Free!* is a labour of love designed to prove that gluten-free food can be excellent.

Rice and Recipes

www.riceandrecipes.com

Recipes, recipe contests, rice links, rice facts.

Gluten Free Foods Direct

www.glutenfreefoodsdirect.co.uk

A family business in North Yorkshire that sells a range of gluten-free products including breakfast cereals, pasta, bread and biscuits, flour, spreads, condiments and frozen foods.

Gluten-Free Diet

www.gluten.net/diet.asp

The Gluten-Free (GF) Diet: The GF diet is the prescribed medical treatment for gluten-intolerance diseases such as coeliac disease (CD) and dermatitis herpetiformis (DH). An immune-system response to eating gluten (storage proteins gliadin and prolamine) results in damage to the small intestine of people with gluten intolerance.

Celiac Disease and Gluten-Free Diet Support Center

www.celiac.com/celiacdisease.html

This support center at Celiac.com provides important resources and information for people on gluten-free diets due to coeliac disease, gluten intolerance, dermatitis herpetiformis, wheat allergy or other health issues. Celiac.com offers key gluten- and wheat-free online resources that are helpful to anyone with special dietary needs.

Gluten Free Foods Ltd

www.glutenfree–foods.co.uk

A mail-order supplier offering a range of over 70 products including cakes, cookies and snacks.

Gluten Free on the go

www.gluten–free–onthego.com

A register of hotels, restaurants, cafés and coffee shops, pubs and takeaways in Britain and some parts of Europe that have signed up to a gluten-free code of practice. The search facility enables you to find a list of suitable venues in an area you are intending to visit, and supplies detailed descriptions, photographs and contact details.

Glutafin

www.glutafin.co.uk

A supplier of gluten-free products, including fresh bread made from gluten-free wheat starch and baked to order. The website includes information on maintaining a balanced diet and a wide range of recipes.

Index

A

C